Copyright ©Simon Bourne 2023

soledoutbook.com

handdyedshoeco.com

The right of Simon Bourne to be identified as the author of this work has been asserted in accordance with the Copyright, Designs and Patents Act 1988.

All rights reserved. No part of this publication may be reproduced, stored in a retrieval system, or transmitted, in any form, or by any means, without the prior written permission of the author.

A CIP catalogue record for this book is available from the British Library

ISBN (Hardback) 978 1 916703 01 8

ISBN (Paperback) 978 1 916703 02 5

Typeset by Eleanor Baggaley

First Published 2023 by Snowdrop Publishing

www.Snowdrop-Publishing.com

Soled Out!

Bankruptcy,
My Greatest Achievement

[signature]

Simon Bourne

To my incredibly patient wife, Lauren, and my beautifully supportive girls, Daisy and Penny.

Thank you.

Foreword

I first met Simon back in 2012 when my husband and I were furnishing the home we'd newly bought in Devon. We'd decided on leather for our sofa, and we wanted it to be a beautiful, classic piece. There are many places closer to home where we might have found such a thing, but once we'd discovered Simon, his love of leather, and the craftsmanship that went into the furniture, we decided we had to go to Newcastle, meet him and see for ourselves. Doubly impressed, we ended up ordering two sofas, not one.

It was a pleasure to get to know Simon as our new sofas took shape. He's smart, engaging and knows his stuff, so I wasn't at all surprised when a few years later, I began to hear of the well-deserved success he was having with his own venture, Hand Dyed Shoe Co. And sadly - because it happened to so many wonderful businesses during the pandemic, and still happens every day to many more - it wasn't a complete shock to learn that his business hadn't come through completely unscathed.

Beyond its humility and relatability, what struck me about Simon's story is that he has the courage to tell it. As we chatted one day about his book, we agreed that whatever the outcome, building a business can be terrifying. As much as our lives as entrepreneurs are filled with ideas, opportunity, and barely-contained excitement, there's another feeling that's all too familiar. It's the one where you're standing on the edge of a precipice, barely able to look down. And it's those mornings that you're ragged and brittle from nights of anxiety and adrenaline, going into days of pressure and expectation. We all have to develop nerves of steel, but sharing the trauma of actually losing your business - that's brave, and important.

His story does many things. It makes some sense of the craziness: If building a business is so stressful, risky, and derailing, why on earth do we do it? Partly, the answer is obvious. Once you hit a certain point, the only way is forward. But it's more than that, and Simon's is a classic tale of how our relationship with our business really is true love. The striving, and belief in the near impossible, the building and creativity, all follow naturally from that.

His story also offers a genuinely helpful, honest account of what happens when things do go wrong. Liquidation, bankruptcy, administrators - we make a point of knowing nothing of these things until we have to. I'm thankful that Simon found a way to share that information in a form that we can take it in, learn from it, admire and support the people who have had to go through it and perhaps - just perhaps - use it for ourselves one day if we have to.

And his story gives hope. Lots and lots of hope. Ultimately it's a story that everyone wants to hear. That you can come back, that there are people who believe in you, love you and will support you. That you, and your business idea, weren't so crazy after all. And that for your family, your friends, your colleagues, your customers and for yourself, you will find ways to pick yourself up and start over again.

Sophie Cornish MBE
Founder, NotOnTheHighStreet

Contents

Introduction	1
1 The End	5
2 The Beginning	19
3 The Jeff Stelling Effect	37
4 The Love of Leather	55
5 Life on the Edge	69
6 Get In The River	83
7 Making a Shoe Guy	97
8 Tipping Point	109
9 Living The Dream	123
10 Return of the Dragon	139
11 Winning	147
12 Dragons' Den	163

13 Growth	175
14 Pandemic	183
15 Loser	195
16 The End	203
17 Liquidation	211
18 The Loss	223
19 Born Again	231
20 Closure	239
21 Distraction	251
22 Home	259
23 Mental Wealth	277
24 Soled Out!	287
25 Redemption	293
Daisy and Penny	307

Introduction

We all strive to protect our children and shield them from the challenges and complexities of adulthood. Safeguarding their innocence and vulnerability in today's fast-paced world filled with peer pressures and expectations is a common parental instinct. During the tumultuous period of losing my business, alongside the harsh reality of declaring bankruptcy, I was no different in my efforts to shield my daughters from the inner turmoil and the arduous processes involved in my financial downfall.

However, there were inevitable moments when I found myself discussing the difficult circumstances with my wife, Lauren, friends, or family members and my girls were unwittingly present. At times, I shared my anguish and thoughts about suicide or discussed the possibility and seeming inevitability of eviction from our home, or how we would find the funds to deal with potential bailiffs. Then, I would suddenly remember that my daughters, aged 8 and 2 at the time, were in the back of the car or just a half-open door away, exposed to my tearful distress and internal crisis.

Society might expect me to feel regret for exposing my children to such difficult experiences, but I don't. I feel remorseful to all those who got caught in the crossfire, but there's a significant difference between remorse and regret. Had I acted completely selfishly or made decisions without considering the impact on others affected by those decisions, then I believe that is different, and regret should play a part in my rehabilitation in life's journey. But I know that I never intended to harm anyone and every decision I made was for the right reasons. I have grown to understand that I never acted out of greed or malice. I didn't engage in cheating or gambling. Every decision I made was guided by what I believed to be the right thing to do, driven by good intentions. I wasn't arrogant or reckless; rather, I was inexperienced, unfortunate, naive, and, at times, foolish. None of these qualities are inherently negative nor something we should spend too much time regretting.

There have been times during the collapse of my business and the ensuing bankruptcy when I did feel regret; plenty of it. This regret for long periods of time choked me as I punished myself for not being financially aware enough or brave enough in my decision-making. For taking gambles or lacking strong leadership. That regret drove me to utter the words 'I'm sorry' countless times and in various ways to many people. But today, my sorrow is exclusive to the pain my lessons brought with them as opposed to the reasons that they came. For that, I'm sorry. I am sorry to my family, my friends and my colleagues, but mostly, I'm sorry to myself. I now understand the importance of self-love. Had I had that lesson before my demise, perhaps those who were caught up in it wouldn't have had to go to work wondering if I would be alive when they returned. For that, I am truly sorry and I vow to never pass on that worry again, no matter how bad things get.

I acknowledge that I made mistakes, and in producing this book, I feel I have taken responsibility for mine and used it to create something positive. Making mistakes is a natural part of the learning process. I also recognise that I did very little wrong, and my primary intent was always to improve the lives of my family. Unfortunate events happen in life, and I didn't aspire to be a millionaire to impress my friends. I aspired to make wealth so that I could give more. That's not something to regret and the aspiration still burns as I write this.

I recognise that most people would prefer to sweep these chilling and horrific memories under the carpet and simply move on. That's what the majority would do. However, for me, I felt that doing that would be the ultimate definition of failure. Failure to acknowledge one's mistakes and take responsibility for them is something I knew I'd carry the weight of for years to come if I didn't do this. Hiding the truth is something to regret. Perhaps publishing a book about your truth is taking it to the extreme. However, in doing so, I can give my girls context when they're old enough to understand what Mummy and Daddy were going through during those unfiltered car journeys. And perhaps that context will help them deal with their own adversity that is inevitably going to be forthcoming in their long lives ahead.

If I can do that with this book, I can sleep at night knowing that I used my experience for good and so, I share this story with you with absolutely no regrets whatsoever.

Simon Bourne
The Shoe Guy

Chapter 1

The End

23rd December 2021. I woke up around 7.20 am. My daughter, Penny, wasn't a great sleeper and inevitably I'd been up a few times in the night. I was tired. Exhausted. The day started in a typical fashion; a long black coffee from the Nespresso machine, a couple of bits of toast and far longer than I should have spent sitting staring out of the dining room window. I did that a lot in recent months and became quite friendly with the local wildlife. I gave most of them names. The robin, which I called Robert, Beryl the blackbird, the array of blue tits along with Paul the pigeon. We gave most of them names - apart from my nemesis, the jackdaws. I'd often talked about shooting them if I could! It was a welcome distraction. I could hear the girls fighting at the top of the stairs so I half-heartedly threw down my anti-depressant tablets and made my way up. I separated the girls and put Daisy in her school uniform. I don't know if it was clean. They both simply had the quickest outfits I could get on them. I don't know if they brushed their teeth. I threw on some old jeans, a crumpled t-shirt from the bedroom floor, and some grubby old trainers that I could vaguely pass as trendy. It was Groundhog Day, a repeat of the same day I'd lived out for most of the last twelve months. The clothes were an outward sign of where my mind was.

As we pulled off the drive, the knots in my stomach were causing me to retch. I looked up at our home, our once beautiful palace filled with hopes, dreams, aspirations and achievements. It looked so spectacularly beautiful and yet, empty. Spectacularly barren. It was overwhelming. The stonework I'd fallen in love with some 18 months prior suddenly looked dirty. It looked revolting. It was a patchwork of fraud, a life I didn't deserve. I stopped looking up, opting instead to look down. It was easier. It was all a lie. I was a fake. I was a loser. I didn't deserve it.

I drove the girls in silence. None of us spoke a word on the seven-minute journey to Grandma's house. I kissed Penny goodbye, avoiding the usual offer of a cup of tea from my mother-in-law, Julie. I asked her if she could pick up Daisy from school later that day before speeding off without so much as a glance backwards.

The only reason I was going to work was to meet Neville Rodgers, a regular customer of Hand Dyed Shoe Co. He was due to visit that afternoon with his son. Neville had spent a few quid over the years with me and by my accounts was a very successful and wealthy man. He would often come in and waste little time racking up four-figure bills by the end of his appointment. Maybe meeting with him could be the answer I was looking for. Then again, I'd been having that thought for a long time, and yet, look at my current situation.

Shortly before 10.00 am, the phone rang. It was my first customer of the day, Louis Hagan. The piercing high-pitched tones of the phone ringing were enough to fill me with dread and discontentment for the hour ahead. I let the phone ring for at least half a dozen rings before I picked it up, hoping he might just hang up himself and fuck off. As I answered the call, I jolted. I snapped into professional mode, fraudster mode, 'Good morning, Hand Dyed Shoe Company...'

That was my first fake of the day. I blundered through the next hour, blabbing, doing my thing and selling him shoes. All this whilst silently praying for him to hurry up. What did it matter, anyway? By this point, I was sure he wasn't going to get his shoes and this whole hour was nothing more than a charade. It was probably the most difficult hour I have had in my life. He'd never have known I was in turmoil. I had become adept at concealing it all in my business. I'd become a professional fraudster.

At 11.30 am, my next customer arrived, Scott Elwell. He was dropping off a pair of shoes he needed repairing. Scott is a great guy; he's passionate about Hand Dyed Shoe Co. and has regularly commented or praised the brand on his social channels or amongst peers. He's passionate about me and would vocalise his admiration for what I'd achieved whenever we met. Naturally, I proceeded into my second fake of the day, laughing and joking. There was no obvious crisis.

'How's business?' I remember he asked. I did the usual, what all business owners do no matter how cloudy the outlook is. I lied and provided an optimistic response. I am sure they train the entrepreneurial response to that question in business schools. I told him it was going 'much better' and that we would soon be back to our pre-pandemic best. I delved into the details of my future plans for the business and watched on as he soaked it all in. We shook hands and he left feeling, like many before him, dosed with optimism for this fabulous brand that he has become deeply inspired by.

As I closed the door. I took what felt like my first breath of that day. It had just gone lunchtime. The winter sun was bursting through the large Georgian sash windows of my studio. It lit up the small leather sofa like a spotlight on a West End stage. Another long intake of breath followed by an even longer exhale. I locked the door.

Now; now was the time. It was *my* time. I was free from distraction and now I was free to do what I'd been craving to do since I opened my eyes that morning. Collapse. Now

I could fall apart. Now, I could mourn.

I steered clear of the sofa and made my way over to the orange leather wingback chair, sitting in a darker, shady corner of the studio. I could feel the draft on my arm, and I slumped down like a pensioner who had lost all bone structure. I opened my phone and began the death scroll. Facebook, Instagram, LinkedIn, Facebook, Instagram ...

Within a couple of minutes, I was jumping back and forth between them all before realising I was only putting off the inevitable; I forcefully put the phone down on the coffee table. It was all but silent; the only noise I could hear was that of another business greeting guests in the corridor outside his studio. I sank further into the chair and let out another deep sigh. I don't think I had ever let out a sigh like that before. I was empty, only this time, I couldn't fill my lungs again. My body was frozen. I began to cry. It wasn't a loud cry or a tearful one. It was an intense grimace, gutsy. My stomach was tighter than a middle-weight boxer. Every muscle in my body grew an inch out of my skin. My belly ached. It felt like it could have taken a thousand kicks from a karate champion without feeling a thing. My shoulders also ached and my hands were sore from gripping the chair's arms as I rocked back and forth. My teeth were tightly clenched. The tears began streaming down my face like a relentless waterfall, but still, there was no noise. My jaw was locked, and my face was rock solid. I was utterly broken.

Suicide had always been an option for me from a very young age. I'd grown up with a father whose mental health had seen him attempt suicide several times. From overdoses to smashing his car into a tree, all before I was six years old. Even today, he still uses the suggestion of suicide as a threat if it will help him to emphasise his point. I had come to believe that if things didn't go well for me, regardless of what 'going well' meant, then I always had suicide as a natural conclusion. In fact, in our early relationship, I used to say to my wife, tongue in cheek, that I didn't think I'd see 40. The underlying truth behind the comment was that I believed suicide would get me before then. Now, here I was, 36 years old, and staring down the barrel.

I'd never considered how I would kill myself. An overdose, which seemed like the most accessible way, seemed too risky - I might die if I took too much, or worse, have some kind of fit and end up in a wheelchair for the rest of my life. Admittedly, it is a strange thought when you're suicidal, not wanting to die, but feeling as if it were the only way out. But it crossed my mind as I convinced myself that now was the time.

Hanging. It was terminal. It was accessible. It was definitive. I could do it in my studio because the ceilings are very high there. Nobody was around. Nobody knew I was even in that room at that specific moment. I looked around the room and there, staring at me as my wife stared at me on our wedding day, was the curtain tieback. A beautiful golden, polyester noose, glittering around a leather curtain, seducing me to walk over and take her into my arms and dazzle around my neck. I stared at it for what felt like hours. I growled at it and began to force air through my teeth, hyperventilating. I was desperate to find the courage. I was screaming at myself inside to get up and go and get the golden noose. *Stop being a coward*, I thought. I was angry with myself for not getting up. I was grappling with my thighs. The reality was, that I knew that if I had lifted myself out of that chair and made the commitment to walk to it, I would be dead. I'd got to that point in life by following that 'commit and do' attitude. If I stood up, I had a choice to make. Do it, or quit. And I knew that I don't quit. I stayed sitting in the chair, taking turns between staring at the noose and then back to the floor. I didn't want to make the choice. I was scared to make it because I knew what I would have committed to. The curdling feeling in my stomach was unbearable. The tears streamed down my face faster and harder. The anger in me was ripping my insides, I could feel my heart beating and my lungs crushing against my rib cage. I was pissed off for bottling it. I was being a coward. I sat for what felt like hours but was probably only around ten minutes, continuing to glare at the golden temptress, willing her to come to me. I wanted the pain to end so badly.

Eventually, whatever there was left inside of me to break, broke. I fell to the ground and curled up into the foetal position. The agony tore through me and I began whaling. Now there was sound. Lots of it. I lay there, yelling to myself. I don't know how long I was there, but I knew one thing for sure, I couldn't let Neville see me like this. That momentary snap of awareness jolted me again. I had to get rid of him.

After a few minutes, I began having a panic attack. I was breathing so fast that I was dizzy and couldn't physically put any weight on my legs. My whole body was shaking, and I felt like my head was bleeding from where I had been yanking my hair. It was as if I were pulling a boat into a dock. I had to compose myself. I had to get rid of Neville.

I hauled myself off the floor and sat up in the chair once more, panting as though I'd just run an Olympic sprint. My hands were trembling as I sent him a text. It read:

> *Neville, I've got so much respect for you I don't think you should come and order shoes from me today. My business is fucked mate. I don't know if you will get the shoes and I don't want to take your money with that anxiety in my mind.*
> *I'm not a well man today and I don't think I can face anybody.*

It's easy to hide behind a text. You don't have to talk

through crying eyes or a ruffled voice. You don't have to read any response. You press send, and that's it. It was done. He was gone. Now what?

I sent another text. It was very unusual for me, typically a man of many words because it read just two. It said,

I'm beat.

It was only two words, but she knew. Lauren's always had this uncanny knack of just knowing how I'm feeling without me having to say much at all. I guess it's because I don't really hide my feelings and I'd rather just say what's bothering me, unlike others who bottle this type of shit up. She's a midwife, working at the Queen Elizabeth Hospital in Gateshead, just outside Newcastle. She was halfway through a 13-hour shift but had found a gap a couple of times that morning to text me. She knew I'd been battling all of this for months, and she told me how proud she was, reaffirming I needed to take one step at a time. I had replied to her earlier messages and told her I was going to do my best and I would see her in the evening when she got home. When she saw the two-word text, she probably knew that something was wrong. Something was different.

She rang me almost immediately. I answered the call but I couldn't speak. I was gagging. I spluttered something like, 'I can't do it.' I can't remember what I said. I think she knew that by 'it' I meant that I couldn't kill myself. She didn't try to counsel me at that moment. She simply told me that she would come to me and she would be with me in 30 minutes. She begged me to 'hang on' until she got there. I promised her I would.

As I waited, I started saying prayers to my late grandad, begging for his help. Grandad was a religious man and without a doubt, his advice would have been to 'find God,' which would fix everything. It did for him. At this moment I think I was willing. I wanted God to come to me. I was willing to do anything that could help. When Lauren arrived, she came in and never spoke a word. I have read of this feeling of safety that others feel in this moment of rescue, but I didn't get that. I was just angry. I wanted to hang myself and now she was there, I knew it wasn't possible. I didn't want her there really and yet, all I wanted was her there. I didn't want her to see me like this. I didn't want to see her like that. I felt bad enough already without seeing the pain she was in too. She hurled herself at me, wrapping her arms tightly around my neck. I hugged her back but it didn't feel much like the many hugs we had exchanged over the previous 19 years. I had no strength left in my arms so I couldn't grip her properly. I weighed around 105 kilos that day, but at that moment I felt that I weighed little more than a toddler. I was so weak. She held me up like I was a rag doll filled with old stuffing.

I barely spoke other than repeatedly murmuring the word

sorry. I felt so sorry I was doing this to her; she didn't deserve it. I was bringing her life into disrepute. I was affecting her career, something she had worked so hard for and cared about deeply. I cared about it too. I made her come out of work to rescue me. I was a selfish, needy, disgusting bastard. I was causing her pain. I felt pathetic and I knew I had let her down - I don't recall her ever having a sick day for herself, let alone for me and my depressing woes. But, she sat, and she did all the things you would expect from a kind, devoted, loving and patient wife. She told me everything would be okay, that she was with me and that we would get through this together as a family. I had little choice other than to agree, although it did just feel like empty words at the time. How could it get better?

Nothing could get any worse for me at this moment. I was so far down the rabbit hole there was very little light left. To make things worse, my phone lit up with a call. The room was well-lit and yet it felt like the light from the phone was enough to illuminate the Universe. The vibration of the phone on the oak coffee table sounded like a thousand wasps crawling around my ears. It was Neville - so I did what most people would do at this moment, I ignored it. Lauren was disturbed. She was very forceful in her opinion that I should answer it. I told her I couldn't face it. I was mad she was even suggesting I should answer it. *Sell shoes, now, like this*, I thought, *you're fucking stupid*. And then it rang again. Lauren reached over me and answered it herself - she'd never spoken to Neville before this moment and he didn't know who she was. She introduced herself through her croaking voice telling Neville I wasn't in a good place. She got up from the chair and walked away from me into the office space around the corner. I could hear them talking and could sense the conversation was suggesting Neville was still coming to see me. The very thought of this almost had me sinking back to the floor - *how could I sell shoes like this?* 30 minutes prior to that moment, all I wanted was a curtain tie around my neck! I couldn't do it. *Was she mental?* I was angry but I had no energy to fight. Lauren and Neville had concluded that he should come.

Cue fake number three. But this time, I couldn't. As Neville walked in, I stood out of the chair to greet him but then almost immediately slumped back into the wing-back, collapsing my eyeline back to the ground. I didn't move. He walked over, placed his hands on my shoulders and said in his thick Northern Irish accent, 'Everything's going to be okay Simon. I'll help you. I've been there.'

After I calmed myself down, Neville took a seat on the sofa, and Lauren made us all a cup of tea. Neville told me that he had been in a situation similar to mine and that he had managed to bounce back from it, not just once but twice. The truth was, at that moment, I didn't know where I stood – I was nothing more than a cash-strapped business owner drowning in debt. The idea of a comeback felt utterly unimaginable. *Come back from what? From where? You can't escape this financial quagmire without losing everything.* I was acutely aware that most of the debt the company owed was tied to me through personal guarantees, given my role as the director of Hand Dyed Shoe Co. Ltd. In essence, it wasn't only the business on the line; my family was also at risk. That's a significant part of what had shattered my state of mind.

Nevertheless, hearing Neville's personal story was inspiring, and it was enough to feed some optimism and bring my emotions back to some kind of rational level. Here was a man of wealth and fortune, a man whom I had on a pedestal as the definition of success, telling me he'd been where I was at that moment. It wasn't a lot, but it was enough to stop me from thinking about the curtain tie for the rest of the day. He handed Lauren four gift cards and told her there was £250 on each of them, spendable in the local supermarket. He insisted we take them, demanding we use them to make sure our girls had a Christmas. It was a gesture beyond words and to this day I feel immense gratitude for it and him. And yet, it wasn't the most important gift he gave me that day. Both he and Lauren, they'd given me a reason to go to bed alive that night. They'd given me a glimmer of hope that things might be okay, somehow.

We picked the girls up from Grandma's house and headed

home. That evening, I found it hard to look at the girls, knowing that earlier that day a huge part of me was very willing to leave them. I held them both tighter than I ever had before and kissed them both goodnight.

Chapter 2

The Beginning

Whenever people ask me to describe myself, one word always comes to mind: I am a dreamer. I love nothing more than achieving extraordinary things; things that either I, or perhaps others, didn't perceive as my destiny. I think about the impossible a lot. But it doesn't stop there; I get obsessed with the impossible, and it doesn't take a lot before I'm working my way towards it. I enjoy fighting and being a little bit under pressure. I produce my best work often when I'm up against it. I am a glass-half-full person, most of the time. Where most people would see difficulty or embarrassment, fear, or nerves, I see challenge and opportunity. I always enjoyed being interviewed, in the same way someone might enjoy standing on stage in front of thousands of people. It was an opportunity to talk about my achievements and my ambitions. I enjoy that sense of belonging. I enjoy inspiring people and seeing them respond to my dreamy nature. Not many things get me more excited than dreams, so if I'm dreaming it, I'm typically selling it. Nerves aren't something I suffer from; they are something I revel in, and I rise to them. I like nerves.

I have always said that Hand Dyed Shoe Co. started long before it became a registered limited company. It's a little bit like a Formula 1 driver who might have started carting at a young age without realising then that their unwitting apprenticeship, along with their surroundings, would develop them into the pinnacle of motorsport. As far back as my teenage years, I can attribute moments in my life as being key factors in forming the idea and subsequently the business.

I was born in January '85 in Scunthorpe, a small North Lincolnshire town famous for its steel industry, which once thrived before its collapse. It wasn't the easiest childhood, but I was always loved. My parents went through a fairly ugly divorce in the early nineties, and my sister, Rachel, and I lived with our dad. There was an arrangement in place that we would visit our mam's house every weekend, alternating between Saturday one week and Friday to Sunday the next.

We lived at 4 Holland Avenue, which I'd politely describe as a run-down council estate. Dad would fix the neighbours' cars on the drive for money. We didn't have a lot, but I wouldn't change it. Rachel and I would play out in the street, and we were safe. All the neighbours looked out for one another. I remember a time when we found our way into a house at the top of our street that seemed abandoned. The garden was full of kitchen appliances, so we decided to take a microwave back down to our end of the street, setting it up like a kitchen around a council bench in the snicket joining us to the next street. We took the kettle and whatever else we could balance on our bikes. We went back and forth several times before Dad caught on to what we were doing. I couldn't tell you why we were doing it; they were just toys. Another time, in the same garden, I found a box full of needles and pills. Fascinated, I coerced Rachel, who was around three at the time, into filling her basket up so we could transport them to the other end of the street, tipping them into a bush behind the wall. There was no logic, and we weren't intentionally being naughty. It was all just play, and we were just being kids. That's the kind of street it was. I look back at those first years of my life with fondness. There was a pureness in Holland Avenue. A sense of belonging.

When I was seven, my dad moved us up to the North East to a small former colliery village called Langley Park, a few miles outside Durham City. He'd met my soon-to-be stepmam, Suzanne. I inherited a brother, Colin, who was almost the same age as me, along with two sisters, Pauline and Lauren, followed by a half-brother, Kieran, who came along in 1994. You can imagine that blending into a new family of six, leaving our mam in Scunthorpe and replacing her with a new version, formed a decent recipe for the stereotypical troublemaker. I was an attention seeker, according to my parents, teachers, and social workers. They weren't wrong. I can only hold my hands up to being the disruptive kid in the class. I'd spend large portions of my school life on report or in isolation for my behaviour. I wasn't consciously seeking attention, but I guess that's what it was. I was boisterous and loud. I was naughty and I was far from easy.

It was that phrase, 'attention seeker' that over the years I can pinpoint as the reason I found my way into business. I've developed strong qualms with the phrase, particularly when it's used to describe a child's behaviour. I often hear it being used when discussing children's behaviour in social groups or among colleagues, and I despise it. Whenever I heard it as a young boy, I felt like there was something wrong with me. I became angry at myself. Everything I did, whether it was good or bad, I punished myself for it. If I got in trouble, I thought it was because I was a bad person. If I was praised, I felt like I was needy or somehow manipulating love from people. I never felt like I deserved to be loved. If anyone ever told me they loved me, I'd often find myself breaking down in tears. At the time, I couldn't explain why, but it was because I didn't feel worthy of love, even at such a young age. I recall my Nana cradling me once as we sat on an armchair together. I was maybe 10 or 11 years old. She was asking me why I was misbehaving so much, and I couldn't answer her. I didn't know why. The moment she said she loved me, I began to sob intensely. I still struggle today to be told I'm loved and to receive that adoration without shutting it down as quickly as I can.

Being called an attention seeker is typically used as a negative description of behaviour. As a child, when you're told you're an attention seeker, you naturally try to understand what it means, and the only conclusion I could come up with was that it means I'm bad. It's a phrase that comes with blame. For me, you can't blame a child for seeking attention; it's entirely normal. All children want and need attention, although some may want and need more than others. There's a simpler and much kinder phrase that I think society could use when describing a child who is perhaps displaying behavioural problems, and that phrase is 'seeking attention.' It's softer and more empathetic, coming from a place of understanding rather than criticism and blame. It begs the question, was I seeking attention? Probably, yes. I surmise I was. I was living in an integrated family of six children, having inherited my new-found brother's bedroom and living space. I probably was seeking attention, and my behaviour, looking back, was fairly normal as I struggled to find my place in this new foreign land.

Over the years, my parents tried all sorts of tactics and support to control my behaviour; counselling, moving me into another bedroom, cuddles, fights, and long talks with my grandparents. The truth is, I know I was trouble, and wherever I went, I would usually end up in some kind of bother. The older I've gotten, the more I've come to understand and accept that my attention-seeking behaviour, or seeking attention, wasn't a flaw in me as it was often put. It's still a part of me now, but it's channelled into the business and used as a positive thing.

While I appreciate that my parents couldn't have afforded it, I sometimes wonder what would have become of me if I had been pushed into football, drama, gymnastics, boxing, or any of the other activities that today's generation of children have so many choices of. Don't get me wrong, I'm not convinced pole vaulting or getting punched in the face would have been my thing. They did try Scouts, St. John's Ambulance, and even karate once, and none of those clubs seemed to straighten me out much. But perhaps if my behaviour had been channelled into something I actually connected with, then maybe it might have helped, and I would have found peace with myself sooner than my early thirties. I don't know.

While I can't say that being labelled an attention seeker was the sole reason for my behavioural problems, I do have a theory as to why I became such a challenge.

I hesitate when I write the word 'traumatic' because some readers may have had challenging childhoods and might consider mine a blessing in comparison. However, when I reflect on my upbringing, I can't think of a better term to describe my feelings today.

Looking back, it seems like I had to grow up too quickly. Leaving Scunthorpe at the age of seven, which I now understand was a blessing, was a traumatic experience for me at the time. Our visits to our mam's house on weekends felt like holidays. Mam would take us to places like Twigmoor Woods with her dog, Bo. We'd dig in the soil and climb trees, and in the winter, Bo would pull Rachel and me on a wooden sledge. We'd go to 'the sandpit,' which was essentially just a sandy patch of land in a field that we found and we would play there for hours on end. We'd pull over at the side of the road to watch combined harvesters collect hay in the summer, and we'd go to the car boot sale most Sunday mornings. We'd visit Mam's friends and play in their gardens and on their computers. Those moments were truly magical.

When we left Scunthorpe, everything changed for Rachel and me. Our routine was upended. I can't recall precisely when it happened, but shortly after we moved to Langley Park and settled into our newly blended family, Dad and Suzanne (my stepmam) gathered us all and decided that we should call Suzanne, Mam, and my dad would be called Dad by my step-siblings. We were compliant and did as we were told, but I instantly felt incredible anxiety about what my biological mother would think. As you can imagine, she didn't like it, and it still pains her today. I understand that my mam (Suzanne) and Dad made that decision with the good intentions of making their new relationship work by fostering unity. I have no doubt now that it was meant well. However, the anxiety I felt that day hints at why my behaviour developed the way it did later on - I was angry, confused, and rebellious.

Simply put, I missed my biological mother, and I utterly despised this new life. I didn't belong here.

My biological parents didn't get along, and neither did my stepmam and stepdad. It was a constant state of animosity, hatred, and volatility. Rachel and I found ourselves caught in the crossfire. Whenever we talked about missing our mam, Dad would quickly shut us down, reminding us that she never wanted us. When we first moved to Durham, we used to meet my mam at Ferrybridge Services at the start of the holidays to spend a week or two with her. Once, our car broke down on the way, leading to utter chaos. Dad was trying to fix the car while Mam and Graham (my stepdad) waited at Ferrybridge. Eventually, Mam and Graham left before we arrived. Rachel and I were distraught. Dad ensured we understood that it was Mam and Graham's fault. According to him, she didn't want us. She never wanted us. She ran off with Graham and left us behind. This is a narrative that persisted as far back as I can remember.

Confused, I used to confront Mam with accusations as

early as eight or nine years old. I was desperate for answers. Tears would stream down my face as I questioned why she didn't want us, delving into the affair between her and my stepdad, with whom I also had a tumultuous relationship. I would challenge her decisions and demand explanations. Her responses were a mix of anger and tears as she shared her version of events. I felt like a malevolent force, making my own mother cry during these interrogations. I carried the guilt of being a 'bad child.' 'Your dad was the one having affairs,' she'd retort. 'He said if he didn't get custody of you, he would kill himself and both of you.' I brought this accusation back home to Durham with me one summer and confronted my dad about it. The situation exploded. They ended up on the phone, engaged in a heated argument. I felt overwhelmed with guilt, torn between two conflicting stories, not knowing whom to believe. It was a distressing experience.

After the Ferrybridge incident, Mam and Graham were either instructed to make the two-hour journey from Scunthorpe to Durham to pick us up for our visit, or they decided to do so themselves. On one occasion, we were set to spend two weeks at Mam's house at the end of the summer break. Rachel and I had been eagerly counting down the weeks and days. However, when they arrived in Langley Park to collect us, a heated argument ensued, and Graham made the painful decision to drive away without us. That day, Rachel and I cried more than I can ever recall. We had spent four weeks of our summer holiday eagerly anticipating our trip to Scunthorpe, only to have it snatched away through no fault of our own, leaving us once again caught in this confusing blame triangle.

The situation deteriorated to the point where they refused to pick us up from our home, so Rachel and I had to walk to the local shop to meet them. I'm not sure if it was because Mam and Dad didn't want them in the street after the previous summer's incidents, or if Mam and Graham didn't want to come into the street themselves. Regardless, it was a clear example of how estranged and challenging the circumstances had become.

By the time I was a teenager, my behaviour had escalated, and I was causing even more problems. I would break things, get into fights, swear and steal. I even resorted to hitting my sisters, spitting, and setting fires in the street. I was banned from the school football team and frequently found myself in detention at school. In my eyes, I was a complete misfit in almost every environment I was in. My medical records even referred to me as *'having a problem, particularly with women and girls.'* While this may have been true in my relationship with my stepmother, I don't recall having specific issues with women. I just seemed to have a problem with everyone, and most people seemed to have a problem with me as well.

I learned a lot from my inquisitive exploration of my biological parents' divorce. By the age of thirteen, I had most of the details about my mam's affair with Graham, my stepdad. I also learned that my dad had affairs with many women and had a gambling problem, particularly with slot machines. He would drink, and often the consequences of that would turn ugly. I remember finding out about the missing spindle on the staircase of our home in Scunthorpe, and how it was the result of a drunken argument. I don't know more than that, but you don't need to be a detective to speculate how that could have happened. I was privy to a lot of information about my parents' private lives. While it wasn't something I wanted to know much about, as I got older and more aware of life, it created more questions and more anger within me. Why? I had so many questions, but I didn't know how to ask them, and when I did, I didn't have the maturity to be able to deal with the answers.

Dad's marriage with my stepmam was, at times, as turbulent as his first. Dad's drinking has never stopped to this day, and it had a significant influence on our home life. Most weekends would descend into very vocal and loud arguments. The six of us would be in bed, but we'd often take turns banging on the floorboards to try to bring an end to the shouting. The arguments were more often than not about the same topic - Rachel and me. Dad would accuse Mam of treating us differently from my three step-siblings, and Mam would accuse Dad of the same. It would often escalate to Dad coming into our room during the night, usually very drunk, to tell Rachel and me that we were leaving. I remember sitting in the car a few times in the early hours of the morning with a hastily packed rucksack. I always thought those arguments were my fault or my sisters'. It was our behaviour that was the problem, and neither Mam nor Dad knew how to deal with the situation.

I blamed my step-parents while growing up. Suzanne and Graham - they were the problem. They were the ones I saw as responsible for why I couldn't have my mam and dad together. They received the brunt of my aggression, which in turn caused more arguments. However, there's no blame now. I look at it all with sadness but without anger. It's a very sad tale. How can you expect a father not to defend himself against an accusation that he threatened to harm me and my sister? Similarly, I know that it was never a case of my mam not wanting us, so it goes without saying that she would want to defend herself against that accusation. We were the unfortunate products of a vile, nasty, and toxic relationship, and sadly, we were just caught in the middle of it all.

Now, having spent most of my life challenging the reasons why things happened, my conclusions are that my biological parents lacked maturity and lived their lives very much hand to mouth. Their own upbringings were turbulent and traumatic in their own rights. They met as teenagers, and I was born when my mam was 22. We lived in poverty. There's no other way of explaining it, and within poverty, you naturally find there are lots of social issues. My dad drank, smoked, and gambled as was the culture we were among. Mam didn't gamble, but she drank and smoked. They were still very much exploring who they were as people, and that spilt over into their private lives. These mistakes developed into affairs, which eventually brought an end to their marriage. My mam left to set up a new life with her new partner, Graham, which my dad felt intolerably bitter about. When he began to fear a custody war, the threats came, which, while unforgivable in many aspects, I do believe they happened, probably in a drunken rant. It's undeniable that my dad loves us, and the one thing he needed in his life was his children. He's still very dependent on us today for him to maintain some form of mental stability. He couldn't lose the fight with my mam - he needed his children for himself - and he made sure he would win by using whatever means necessary. My dad was eventually arrested sometime around 1990-1991 and detained under the Mental Health Act, and we lived with my aunty and uncle for a while whilst things settled down. Eventually, Mam relinquished the fight, and Dad was awarded full custody of Rachel and me.

It's difficult to understand how an alcohol abuser with a medically diagnosed mental health condition could win custody in court. I do feel that had Mam fought even a little bit, she would have won custody of us in court, which I think adds credence to Dad's theories as I grew up. But it wasn't a case of Mam not wanting us. Graham didn't, and my mam has never had the ability or heart to fight anyone, particularly men. More often than not, she has taken the easy route, rather than the right route, which is why my dad won the battle.

You may have heard the expression of one person's truth and another person's truth, and then there's the truth. I might not have my conclusions entirely right, but they're certainly my truth, and I doubt they're far wrong.

Eventually, we moved to Durham. On paper, it was a cruel move to take us far away from our mother and the arrangement that was in place by the courts. However, Dad wanted a family. He wanted a wife. He wanted to get away from Scunthorpe, and he fell in love with Suzanne, my stepmam, eventually marrying. That scenario came with a new postcode 150 miles north of Scunthorpe, so we moved. The marriage was difficult and, for me, lacked true togetherness. Perhaps the pressure of six young personalities with different needs was quite simply too much to bear, and eventually, it broke. Suzanne, whom I blamed a lot as a youngster, I actually blame the least today. I'm exceptionally proud to call Suzanne my mam today. She gave me structure and professional ambition. It was Mam who taught me about hard work and believing in yourself to outgrow your perceived destiny. She was a midwife when we first met in 1992, before retraining at college to become a Health Visitor in the late '90s. Mam's divorce from my dad in 2002 is, for me, the saddest thing about my life. I wish they could have worked out because that marriage was the best thing my dad has ever had. He abused it with alcohol and took it for granted until eventually it was destroyed, and the pattern he chose in his life has continued to this very day.

My understanding today is that all my parents did their best, and their intent was always good, even if certain choices weren't. It's nothing more than sad that childhood for me simply couldn't have been what I would have wanted it to be, and as a result, I suffered. The emotional adult I am today was equally so as a child, and that manifested itself into bad behaviour and seeking attention, which when managed turned into insecurity. I didn't have the maturity or understanding to be able to open dialogue like I am able to today.

Managing a young stepfamily is a delicate dynamic, and I imagine it takes an awful lot of self-control, discipline, and reflection to remain balanced and unbiased. I'm not sure I could do it. It took me the best part of thirty years to accept and understand the reasons, psychology, and circumstances. It took the same amount of time for me to forgive myself for being an attention seeker. I was probably always going to be a little bit mischievous, but if we're looking for an understanding of why I was, and to some extent still am, seeking attention, I think the answers lie within my childhood. Everybody did their best, including myself. There is no trauma, not anymore. I am grateful. Gratefulness is my power. It is because of this backstory that Hand Dyed Shoe Co. has gone on to become what it is. So, for me, I became an entrepreneur in 1990, when I was five years old, my parents divorced, and my inner demons began.

The narrative of my destiny really began to change in the summer of 2002. I met my wife-to-be, Lauren Turnbull. She was 15, and I was 17. She wore pink pedal pusher trousers and a black vest top. She was super slender with tiny hips and a delicate dimple in her chin. Her hair was down past her shoulders, dark brown, and slightly curled. She had deep chocolate brown eyes and probably the palest white skin I've ever seen. She was gorgeous, but it wasn't love at first sight. It couldn't have been, because I loved most girls who said hello to me at first sight, which retrospectively tells me that I had no idea what love was that day. We met in the local shop buying ice creams on a red-hot summer's day and spent most of the rest of that day chatting. I take great pride in writing that she got my number first, and she will laugh when she reads this. I didn't know it at the time, but it was one of those sliding doors moments. Without that day, I wouldn't have written this story.

I left secondary school in 2001. My greatest success at school was getting a B grade in English Literature and a C in English Language. I attribute much of my success to my teacher, Mr Crabtree, who, for some reason or another, had placed me in the top class for the subject when it came to our choices. He was one of the teachers I respected quite a bit, likely because I was in the top class and felt that came with a sense of responsibility. I put in a lot of effort in my English classes because I wanted to please Mr Crabtree.

Overall, I left school with 3 GCSEs graded A-C, while the rest were all grade D. I later resat my maths at New College Durham and earned a BTEC National Diploma in Sports Studies. However, before pursuing further education, I dropped out of two apprenticeships; one in Business Studies with G&A Kitchens after I accidentally wrote off their ride-on lawnmower, and the second as a car mechanic with Fred Henderson's garage. At that time, I had no clear direction or idea of what I wanted to do, so I went to college as a way to avoid entering the real world, enjoy playing football, and pursue romantic interests.

After college, I had a job working for an early version of what would later become JD Sports, known then as First Sport. I distinctly remember meeting John Wardle, the individual who founded the company. I must admit I was a bit starstruck, although not so much because of his entrepreneurial achievements, but more that he was also on the board at Manchester City Football Club. Anything related to football would certainly capture my attention.

Chapter 3

The Jeff Stelling Effect

During my twenties, I was employed by Durham County Council. I began in their finance department and later transitioned into a marketing role within the Children and Young People's Service. Outside of work, my life revolved around football. I may not have had the skill to play at a high level, but I could easily recite statistics for a random Australian player competing in the Indian second division without hesitation. Lauren often found it astonishing how much useless football-related information I retained.

As I reached my mid-twenties, I started to contemplate my career path. I pondered what I truly loved and excelled at. Writing stood out to me as a creative outlet, and I had a passion for football. It became apparent to me that I should pursue a career as a football journalist.

I seldom skipped a Saturday, and I was a dedicated viewer of Jeff Stelling and his colleagues on Sky Sports News. It wasn't long before an idea struck me, and I set a clear goal for myself: I wanted to secure a job that would allow me to travel the world while getting paid to discuss and write about football.

I don't know if you've ever tried to launch a new career in an industry where you have zero qualifications or reputation. I applied for so many jobs, but they all wanted an NCTJ qualification - something I obviously didn't have. Given that I needed to work to pay my rent, etc. I couldn't afford to study. Nevertheless, I persisted.

In early 2007, I re-enrolled at college; this time, it was an adult creative writing course. I was overqualified for it really; many of the other students were there as some kind of job seekers' enforced punishment - the government hoping that by offering these individuals some education, they would be able to move on to better things. Many of them couldn't write at all, let alone creatively, but I attended every week all the same. What I was getting out of it was simply a reminder of the basics: where apostrophes should go, how to correctly use grammar and that sort of stuff. I forget the lecturer's name, but I remember she really enjoyed my work. We wrote some poetry one week, and that was something I always enjoyed - playing with words to make them rhyme. I used a lot of metaphors in my poetry. I remember, our last assignment was to write a nonfiction story, and it would be assessed and marked. You would only get a pass or fail, and by this point, I knew I wouldn't fail; I was the lecturer's star writer after all. Yet, it didn't stop me from putting in the effort.

The piece I wrote was around ten pages long; the story of Rita, a down-to-earth northern woman who found herself caught up in an adulterous affair with a taxi driver, only for her husband to find out. It was pretty dark; domestic abuse, self-harm, and suicide all featured. It was creative, all right, and I passed. Not before my lecturer passed a comment on the topic, probably wondering if I was all right in the head.

On the back of finishing college, I felt much more confident with writing. I started to reach out for voluntary work, beginning with writing the match reports for my own Sunday League football team. I published them on a website I created for our team, Hamsteels FC. My first proper publication came quite close to home - my old hometown, Scunthorpe. I targeted the matchday programme for Scunthorpe United. For me, getting an article in the Scunthorpe United matchday programme would be like an actress landing her first gig on Broadway, so I really focused on how I was going to do it. I decided that my way in was to write the piece before I asked - most of my rejections previously were based on the fact I was speculatively pitching rather than presenting my work.

As I explained earlier, my memory of footballers' careers is remarkably weird, and for whatever reason, this guy popped into my mind: Ashley Fickling. If you did a Google search for Ashley, I'm sure he'd forgive me for saying there wouldn't be a lot you'd find. Perhaps a brief Wikipedia page. But for me, that was great. It meant there were so many unanswered questions. What is he up to now? Scunny fans would want to know this. I set about tracking him down, contacting Scarborough, his last known club. They replied, which encouraged me further. They told me to contact Sheffield Wednesday, where they said he was briefly a physio for the youth teams there. So, I did. And they replied with his telephone number. He was still a physio for their youth team!

Christ almighty. I had the number for a footballer! A real footballer. One who had played for my club! I look back now, and I do laugh. I don't think I'd be so starstruck by a Division Three footballer these days, but at the time I was young, and it felt like a big deal. I did what people under 30 would do at the time; I sent him a text. I still do this today, hiding behind text messages and emails. I quite like the soft approach; I don't like to bother people. He replied and told me the club had informed him that I might be in touch, and we arranged a suitable time for me to call. That evening, I prepared myself. I borrowed a Dictaphone from work so I could record the call, and I prepared my questions. When he answered, I was so nervous, but I played it cool with what I hoped came across as effortless nonchalance. I told Ashley I was a journalist working for Scunthorpe United, which of course I wasn't, but I was hoping that this interview might lead to that coming true. He was modest, wondering why anyone from Scunthorpe would be interested in his onward career. I mean, I thought they would be, but now I don't know...

The interview lasted about thirty minutes, and by the end, I had my recording. I set about turning it into a story - the story of Ashley Fickling. It was around 300 words long. I asked Lauren to proofread it for me as well as a couple of friends. They signed off on it and told me it was great, so I sent it in. A day went by, then another, and then another. Nothing. The next home game came and went, and I heard nothing. I was gutted. It set me back quite a bit; I assumed that the programme editor must have thought it was terrible, and that was that. My fingers ached from the persistent refreshing of my inbox. *It's that stupid NCTJ, isn't it?* I thought to myself. Over a week went by before it came - the dreaded rejection email. I could see in the preview, *Hello Simon, I am sorry...'* it said.

I had to gear myself up to read it, so I didn't immediately open it. When I did, I wished I had sooner!

Hello Simon,

I am sorry I have not replied to your message sooner. I was extremely busy editing the programme for last weekend's game and I just didn't get around to it.

The article with Ashley Fickling is excellent and

I would love to use it in the programme for our next game against Tranmere if that is okay with you.

Kind regards,

Chris Mumby,

Programme Editor, Scunthorpe United.

Wow! My work. My article. It was going in my club's matchday programme. Thousands of people were going to see my name in that programme. Realistically, hardly anyone would notice the name of the journalist other than me, but you know what I mean. It was such an incredible feeling, and one, even today, I still smile about when I think of it. The 13th September 2008. I framed it once I received my complimentary copy from Chris in the post, and I still have it.

Journalism became a massive part of my spare time. I wrote several more articles for Scunthorpe United and the following season, Chris asked me if I would like a permanent slot in the programme. You bet I did! I interviewed so many footballers of yesteryear that season, including some of my absolute heroes growing up. Guy Ipoua, a Cameroonian forward who began his career at Atletico Madrid and bagged 23 goals for The Iron across two seasons bridging the millennium. Lionel Pérez, the French goalie probably best remembered for being chipped by Eric Cantona while playing for

Sunderland. I began contributing to other programmes too. Newcastle United had me do a piece with Barrie Thomas, a striker from the 60s who played for both Scunthorpe and the Magpies. I wrote for Sunderland and Middlesbrough; I was living my dream, but there was one problem. It wasn't my job, and none of it paid anything.

One of my favourite memories came about in 2009 when I decided to take three weeks out of work and travel to India. I'd never been beyond Spain before that, so the thought of going to India, on my own, was a bit odd among friends and family. But it was that oddness that attracted me to it. I made it my business to combine my travelling with some work. There was a tournament called the Nehru Cup being played that summer. I don't recall how I managed it, but I arranged accreditation before I got to Delhi. I had connected with a journalist online, and he helped me with what I needed to do. I picked up my pass and made my way to the ground. India versus Lebanon at the Ambedkar Stadium, New Delhi. I wasn't working for anyone other than myself. But I was there, in New Delhi, in a football stadium, as a fully-fledged journalist. I was there for the press conferences and the post-match interviews. It was crazy. I made it to the final too, with India winning on penalties against Syria. I still can't quite believe this happened sometimes.

With my Scunthorpe work progressing and India ticked off, I began to think back to my goal - to get onto Soccer

Saturday - and questioned how I could get there. I began tuning in with extra interest, watching the names of the reporters who were at the grounds while Jeff Stelling was doing his thing. I hit Google, searching their names to see if I could find contact details, and found that one of them had his own website. His name was Stuart Jones, a journalist from the Midlands. His website shared many of his contributions to all sorts of publications and broadcasters. He had a keen eye for golf as well as football.

I began writing my email, attaching grainy scanned images of my printed articles and boasting about my contributions. I had built my own website by this point, www.simonbourne.co.uk, and my email address was greatideas@simonbourne.co.uk. It was my ambition to work for Soccer Saturday and Jeff Stelling. I thought I looked and sounded like a professional journalist.

Stuart was quite a condescending chap. I felt like he got a bit of a kick out of being on Soccer Saturday. His ego enjoyed it, I think. But perhaps I wrote that because my ego took a big knock when he replied. He pulled me up on a couple of typos in my email, called out the incorrect use of speech marks in my articles, and pretty much criticised my website. Charming, I thought. Despite the criticism, he held the key to my dream, so I took it on the chin, apologising for the mistakes. Needless to say, I triple-checked everything before I replied!

I was desperate to know how he got the job working for Sky Sports. I needed to meet Stuart in person, so I asked him if I could maybe join him at one of his games sometime soon. I'd love to watch him and see how it all worked. Unfortunately, he said he couldn't help with that because I would need media accreditation, and only those working for the media could get it. But he did agree to meet me. And what better place to meet than Glanford Park, home of Scunthorpe United!

I finished work early on a Tuesday evening, making my way down the A1, a two-hour drive to Scunthorpe from Durham. I'd agreed to meet Stuart in the café at Tesco, just over the road from the ground. As I walked in, David Moyes, the Everton manager, was sitting at the table beside me. I was completely in awe. I didn't dare speak to him. Thankfully, he left before Stuart arrived, and I managed to recompose myself to meet him.

Stuart was never visually on TV; it was just his voice describing the goings-on at usually lower league football games, so I didn't know what he looked like. It was one of those moments when he came in, where he spoke, and you get a bit shocked because you know the voice but it feels weird seeing it come out of someone's mouth whom you don't know. We sat down for around thirty minutes before Stuart had to be at the ground ready for the show, and he went through his journey. It was similar to mine; lots of volunteering, rejection, and pitching. He had done a lot of work for local radio in the Midlands where he lived, and that's how he managed to get into the broadcasting side of things, picking up a match report gig for a local station. I think he was impressed by the fact I had driven two hours just to meet him for a thirty-minute chat because soon after the full-time whistle went, he emailed to say he would be in touch. Not much more than that.

A couple of weeks passed, and he wrote again. He told me he had an opportunity for me. It was working for ITV. It was unpaid, of course. The job was to do post-match interviews with the managers and players at Guiseley in West Yorkshire on the back of their FA Cup First Round tie with Barrow. The footage, if chosen, would feature on ITV's version of Match of the Day that night. This was it; this was my audition for Soccer Saturday!

Midweek came, and I received my media accreditation pass in the post. *Simon Bourne, ITV* it said on it. Wow! I set off around three hours before kick-off on the hour-and-a-half drive. If you've ever been to a non-league football stadium, they aren't much like the Premier League grounds you see on TV most weeks. Guiseley's ground looked like my local village pitch. It had a stand on one side with the other three ends open for standing. A good few hundred fans were in when the teams emerged from the wooden shack changing rooms. As the game kicked off, I was so nervous.

I was shaking. *What if my batteries die in my Dictaphone,* I panicked. *What if I stutter? What if I ask the wrong question? Stuart will kill me.* I felt so much pressure, and I blew it.

The full-time whistle came, and I didn't know where I was supposed to go. The game finished 0-0, it was rubbish. The players left the pitch with the managers and went into the changing rooms. The fans left, and I just stood about, waiting to see what would happen. I had a cameraman with me - I think it was his first rodeo too. We scurried our way over toward the cabin and waited for someone to come out. One of the players emerged, and so I asked him if the managers would be coming out soon because I needed to get an interview with them. Stuart Kittrick came first, Guiseley's manager. The first thing I asked him was, 'Can you sum that one up for us, Stuart?' It was a terrible question because it was the worst game of football I think I'd ever seen. *How could anyone sum it up?* But anyway, he began to. I wasn't listening, only focusing on what I should ask him next and when. I think I asked maybe two more questions before I thanked him. As he left, I felt almost tearful. The pressure was too much. I completely buckled, and I told the cameraman I was done and leaving. To this day, I regret that decision.

I felt sick driving home. I didn't get the interview. ITV would never want me again. Stuart would be done with me. When he called, I lied. I told him the Barrow manager was raging and refused to do an interview. Stuart couldn't understand it, having read a match report online from some other journalist. There was no mention of any argument, so why wouldn't he do an interview? 'He just said he wouldn't,' I persisted. I know he didn't believe me, rightly so, but what more could he say?

Heaven knows what happened when he told ITV. I tuned in to ITV's highlight show that evening at 11.30 pm. I waited with bated breath through all the first-round ties, and unsurprisingly, the Guiseley game was virtually last on. I think they showed maybe two shots from the game, and they didn't bother with the Kittrick interview. I wasn't surprised, but I was so disappointed. I knew I'd let myself down. I promised myself that if I got another shot, I'd make sure I got the interview, even if it was terrible.

A year passed by before I heard anything again from Stuart about a reporting gig. But he did call again. 'I've got another gig for you,' he told me. I couldn't believe it. 'You're going to like this one! How are you fixed on 10th November?' I didn't know how I was fixed, but I told him I was free. 'Great,' he said, 'Blundell Park, Grimsby Town versus Scunthorpe United. Put it in your diary; make sure you get an interview with both managers.' Can you believe that? My second gig for ITV. I was going to do a post-match interview with Brian Laws, Scunthorpe United legend, and manager of the club for over a decade, and not only that, we were playing our local rivals in a big North Lincolnshire derby. I couldn't believe my luck!

I travelled down and got to Grimsby (actually Cleethorpes; if you know, you know) around two hours before kick-off. Blundell Park is a much bigger ground than Guiseley's, and they had a proper media entrance. It was amazing, strolling past the fans and through the central doors where the players come in, making my way to the media lounge. Now, when I say lounge, I am overselling it a bit. It was a pokey room, a bit like the caretaker's office at your old school, and in the corner was a plate of cheap ham sandwiches. I didn't know if you had to buy them or not, so I didn't have any.

The game kicked off, and it was noisy, with both sets of fans - all locally born and mostly from working-class backgrounds - hurling abuse left, right, and centre. I heard a few racist remarks in the crowd, but even then, in 2013, it wasn't something that was talked about like it is today. It was that kind of game. Unfortunately for me, though, it finished 0-0, again! Can you believe it? I did, however, get the interviews. Firstly, Paul Hurst, a Rotherham United legend doing a decent job with The Mariners, followed by my guy, Brian Laws. It was such a proud moment for me, and I had it on camera! The interview started ropey as I stuttered my way past my first question. Brian, perhaps sensing my nerves, I don't know, did me a favour and talked for around a minute in his answer. The second question fell out, and then a few after that. I was a relieved man by the end of it, but a very proud one at that. I had done it.

Sadly, for me, it didn't make the highlight reel on ITV once again as the bore draw was eclipsed by a few 1-0 thrillers. Never mind, I'd try again next year. However, this time, I didn't have to wait so long. The next week Stuart called to say he had another job for me, and this time, it was paid. I'd never earned a penny from any of the articles I'd written. I'd even sandwiched in a week in Brighton working for free for a new football magazine while taking annual leave from my job; the highlight being interviewing K'Naan, a Somalian rapper about his (pretty awful) World Cup song. I'd travelled to meetings, travelled to Guiseley and Grimsby, I'd spent a lot of money on petrol, trains, and buses trying to get to this point. The gig would pay me £30. It was for Absolute Radio, a new station that was quickly emerging on the digital radio scene.

I had to attend a press conference at Sunderland's training base, where Martin O'Neal (the club's manager) was due to speak. Now, this was a real eye-opener. As I entered the room, I instantly felt like a tuna fish in a sea of sharks. A blonde-haired, fuzzy-faced youngster amongst grown men. Proper journalists. Real journalists with NCTJ qualifications. I was petrified. I was there, like the others, to get Martin's thoughts on the forthcoming fixture, and in truth,

I didn't need to do anything because the other guys just took control. I put my dictaphone on the table in front of Martin, walked away to my seat, and just sat, listening to the other boys asking him questions. I was itching to ask something. I wanted to ask him if he thought Lee Cattermole was close to getting a call-up for England, but I bottled it, again. At least this time, it wasn't my job to ask questions.

I got home and sent the footage over to Absolute. A few days later, Stuart sent me my £30. I was thrilled! My first paid journalism gig.

A few more of these arrived over the next year or so. I interviewed Steven Taylor, Newcastle's centre-half who was in the prime of his life at the time and was being talked about for England in the press. Fabricio Coloccini, who won 39 caps for Argentina and played under Diego Maradona at the 2010 World Cup. Cheick Tioté, an Ivory Coast international player who sadly died a few years ago while playing in China. I attended more press conferences, and while I never needed to ask a question myself, eventually I did ask Alan Pardew if he thought his Newcastle team was mentally tough enough to withstand their push for European football. I picked up some work with Setanta Sports doing written match reports for their website, which meant I pretty much enjoyed a season ticket for football in the North West. I travelled most Saturdays to Manchester, Liverpool, Bolton, Blackburn, or Burnley and enjoyed collecting my £30 each

Monday. I started to get the supporters' bus to games, sitting with the fans when the North East clubs were playing away. This reduced my travel costs and the financial burden I was putting on myself to do the job. I loved that season. The press room at the Etihad Stadium is a little different from the caretaker's closet I enjoyed at Blundell Park, mixing it with Soccer Saturday and TalkSport reporters. David Craig, Matt Murray, Iain Dowie, Ally McCoist. I enjoyed a satisfying heart-to-heart with Danny Mills, a former England international, in the press room at Old Trafford once about what it was like playing in a major tournament for your country. I was in my element, and I was progressing. Although Stuart didn't think so - or at least he didn't make me feel like I was.

Outside of broadcasting, I continued my slot with Scunthorpe United's programme and began working for a website called Football Friends, a site whose mission to build a community of fans through exclusive content became my mission, and I took a front seat in driving content.

All of this, everything I was doing, the hours I was spending writing, recording, and travelling was outside of my full-time job, by this point in marketing for the local council. It was all with one focus in mind: getting on Soccer Saturday.

On 18th August 2012, Lauren and I were married. We'd been together for ten years on the day we got married. By that November, she was pregnant with our firstborn, Daisy Vee Bourne. I suffered quite badly from anxiety while she was pregnant, wondering if I was cut out to be a father. *I'm too selfish. I'm too lazy. What if I don't love the baby the way everyone tells you that you will?* All regular thoughts.

A few weeks after we found out she was pregnant, I was offered voluntary redundancy from my marketing job with the local authority. They offered me £2,300, or I could be repositioned in another team. I decided to take the money, feeling it was a good opportunity to devote more time to journalism and try to increase my earnings. It was about two months of wages, so I had a bit of time to work out my next move, although when I look back now I realise two months is not a long time at all.

Alongside my journalism, when I wasn't doing match reports and post-match interviews on a Saturday, I'd been doing a bit of work for a local furniture company called The Original Sofa Company. I blagged the work while buying a sofa there, telling David Robinson, the owner, that I could help with their marketing and sales. I had no idea if I could, but after a bit of badgering, he invited me in one weekend. After about fifteen minutes or so of explaining the pricing, he left me to it - I wrote him a blog for the website, took a few photos, and gratefully took his £50 for the day's work.

Here I was, fast approaching my thirties. My dreams had

taken me to some of the biggest football grounds in Britain. It had seen me collecting press passes from five-star hotels in India, and mingling with some of the best sports writers from around Asia. I'd been published in magazines, and my club's programme and was being sounded out for work with major broadcasters such as ITV and Setanta Sports.

And yet, I'd spent thousands of pounds doing it and was no nearer to making a career out of it. I never made it onto Soccer Saturday. So, was it worth it? Was I successful?

My answer to that question is always very simple. I was more successful than all those before me who simply dreamt it.

Chapter 4

The Love of Leather

The Original Sofa Company was a bit of a mixed bag in terms of its product offering. Boasting arguably the largest collection of second-hand and vintage Chesterfield furniture in the country, we specialised in restoring old pieces back to their former glories - but not so much so that we lost all that natural and authentic character.

Aside from restored Chesterfields, we also made them, and these were, for me, the finest Chesterfields you could buy anywhere in the world. Crafted in three 'manners,' we had several price points going right up to our incredible Manner One, a handmade, hand-dyed leather Chesterfield crafted entirely in 19th-century methods. Horsehair fillings, solid beechwood framework, hand-tied loose coil springs. Over 160 hours of craft in one single sofa and a juicy £12,000 minimum price tag.

Bear in mind that I had never spent more than £500 on a sofa - my sofa came from Argos out of the catalogue - this was another world to me. I was playing with some really big people, and you know what, I bloody loved it! It wasn't long after I left the council that I managed to convince David to take me on full-time. I was relieved because it also wasn't long before I realised I wasn't suddenly going to find a £20k salary in journalism without that darn NCTJ qualification. Nevertheless, this new life in the private sector was exciting.

In my early twenties, I recall sitting down with my dad one day when I was out of work and suggesting that I liked the idea of starting a company - my own business - helping people write CVs and doing general computery stuff. I was always handy on a computer, designing things, researching the internet, and spreadsheets. That kind of thing. Dad played it down and told me that it wouldn't work. He was right; it wouldn't have happened back then. However, it took a good few years before I entertained any other ideas again. The irony of wanting to start a CV writing business when I didn't have a job is admittedly somewhat amusing.

My first dabble in making money outside of a job was with a little idea I had called 'The Website Writer'. We had a digital bulletin board at Durham County Council, an Intranet kind of thing where you could post about personal items you were selling or looking for. They also had another section that allowed you to advertise your business, if you had one. I looked every day and was always trying to think of what business I could post on there. Alongside my journalism, I built a website for my football team, Hamsteels Inn, along with the site for my journalism. I'd done it using some template hosting software called Mr Site. I figured I could make good money making sites for other council workers who were running their own little enterprises, so I started selling them my skills for £150 per website. It would take me hours, days even by the time I had finished it, trained them how to use it and fixed complications. I wasn't fussed though; £150 was a lot of money to me back then, so it was always rewarding to get paid. For a while, I thought this was me set for life! I created a logo and designed some training guides for my clients, all professionally branded up, or so I thought, in those plastic punch wallets. It was a decent little gig, but after a while, I got bored of it and found it was taking up too much of my time, so I let it quieten off and eventually disappeared. The Website Writer was long before I met David Robinson, but I look back now, and I think I was probably showing early signs of someone with an eye and a flair for business.

David is a cool guy, full of charisma. He's from Sunderland, but you wouldn't know it to talk to him. I remember him recounting his elocution lessons to me once; something I didn't even know existed. He's incredibly dapper and handsome and he drove a 1998 Porsche 911. His aftershave was always very expensive, and he bought most of his clothes from Tom Ford, Gucci, or Selfridges. David is the king when it comes to quality. Quality furniture. Quality wine. Quality cars. Quality house. He likes the finer things in life, and fair play to him. I loved working for him. I was so eager to please him, and there was little that gave me greater joy than to call or text him to say I'd sold a sofa. I was so eager, that in the summer of 2013, after a bumper sales month, I earned my first-ever pay packet over £2,000. With it, I bought a private registration for my car, S111 OSC. I did it as a show of my dedication to the brand and if I'm honest, because I wanted David to love me even more. He heaped me with praise, and I craved it so much. I was spending more and more time in the evenings trying to coerce customers into parting with their cash on one of these fine pieces of art - a handmade, hand-dyed Chesterfield sofa. It wasn't long until David just left me to it. I loved it. It was my business as well as his - although it wasn't mine on paper or at Companies House, I didn't care one bit. I started reconstructing elements of the business as much as David would allow. I'd tweak the website, playing around with new layouts and alternate photography. The social channels were, for me, what I imagine a room full of blank canvases might have felt like for Picasso. It was my playground to creatively experiment. I redeveloped our production planner, trying to influence the workshop and improve our abilities to plan work while keeping a customer informed and in truth, at bay with their demand for information. A new piece of software I found for the website enabled us to instantly chat with our website visitors, massively improving our chances of conversion. But most of all, I loved our customers. I buzzed them. When sales were coming in, I was at my happiest. We were making money, David was happy and feeding my ego, and I was doing my favourite thing, communicating with humans. I still shudder today at the notion that I'm a great salesman because of the stereotype that the term comes with, but the reality is, that I am. I have a natural ability to build relationships with people and match a client's personality to a product by little more than intuition. I've been on training courses where they say don't judge your client and while I get it, I think the best salespeople do judge their clients; they just judge them well. What I mean is you don't want to be trying to flog a battered old Chesterfield to someone who is looking for luxury. And most of all, you don't want to be flogging anything at all until you have that customer's trust.

The Original Sofa Company (OSC) became my life, and David became my unofficial mentor and inspiration. He was everything I wanted to be. He had the watch, the car, the beautiful family, the house, the lifestyle, the wine, the social circle, the charm, the looks. How did David do it? I'd spend most of my nights falling asleep thinking about how David Robinson became so rich and so good at what he did.

By now, the journalism work was dwindling. I was becoming tired of Stuart and travelling up and down the country for £30, losing money when I could be making it on my doorstep with OSC. There was a time in my life when money didn't matter because my love and ambition were burning so brightly that I just didn't care. But I knew I was losing my drive for it. Stuart asked me to cover a game one weekend, Everton v Blackburn at Goodison Park. Post-match interviews and a match report. He could pay me £35. I turned it down and made a lame excuse. I just wanted to be at OSC. I was becoming more and more influenced by David, and I was spending more time thinking about his life and his company than I was about sports journalism.

I was thinking a lot about how I could make money like him. *How can I give my family a similar life to what David gives to his? What could I do to one day own a Porsche?* One idea I had was really cool, and I still think there could be a market for it. I'd just become a father, and when we were looking for a cot for our imminent arrival, I was very uninspired. I like quirky things, things that are unique and different, and my house was already filled with lots of oddities and treasures. All the cots looked like wooden cages. I found an old art deco cot on eBay and fell completely in love with it. I travelled from Durham to Ipswich, over 250 miles, to collect it. It was amazing. The base was made from a steel net-like structure, and the side of the cot folded down. The head and footboards were sculpted with beautiful spindles and curves. I loved it, but there was one problem. It was lathered in lead-based paint. I took it to a professional paint-stripping company and had the old paint removed from the wooden frame. When I got it back, I painted it sunshine yellow in baby-friendly paint. It looked incredible. I was so excited about it.

The business was a clone of David's. We'd buy old cots and restore them, and we'd make new ones in 19th-century styles. We would redesign the cot industry. And it would be called Restoration Baby!

Like before, I built a website, got some cots, restored them, and took them out on a photoshoot. Some of the photos were super cool. However, it quickly became apparent that the lead paint thing was a massive problem. Combined with the time it was taking to physically paint them to a good standard worthy of selling them on; it was a non-starter. I had a long chat with Trading Standards about the idea, and that was enough to put me off the idea. Restoration Baby never made it to Companies House.

One thing that caught my interest, though, was photography. David had a Nikon camera, and we used it in the showroom and workshop to create content for the website and social media. I never quite got the hang of it, and so, to improve my skills and further impress David, I enrolled in an adult photography course at Gosforth High School. I loved it. A bit like when I did the creative writing course in my early twenties, I was probably a little overqualified. I knew my way around the camera, and the first few lessons were teaching people how to put batteries in it, so I was a little bit bored, to say the least.

Nevertheless, I stuck with it for the full 16 weeks, and I never missed a lesson or a photography excursion. I could tell that my tutor, Bill Bradley, liked my work. He gave me a bit of extra attention and was very helpful when it came to setting up my new Sony A300 camera. Each week, we were all given a project to photograph something, and I'd naturally never take things as simple as they were meant to be. 'Next week, I want you to bring in a photograph of some water,' Bill said one week. I organised for my mate to come down to my house, and we spent nearly three hours poking and prodding his eyes until we got a tear. That was my water.

At the beginning of every class, we would go through everyone's photos, and the class, along with Bill, would review the composition and the data from behind the shot. I hate to hide my modesty, but my work was worlds apart from the rest of the class. I knew I had a bit of talent. Naturally, I can't just rest at that. I had to do something with it, and so not long after the course concluded, I set up Langley Portraits Photography. My favourite thing to take photos of was people, so I did a couple of shoots with friends to build up a portfolio. I had people in rivers, up trees, in vintage dresses, and even tested out a little boudoir shoot once! I was thoroughly enjoying it. But, if I was to make some money from this, I needed to do weddings, so I set about faking a wedding for that all-important sales pitch. I picked up a second-hand wedding dress from a charity shop and coerced Lauren into playing model for the day. We went up to a local church, and we shot pictures all day. Lauren would never agree, but she could be a model. Her hair is golden orange, and she has a natural, pale complexion. She's tall and thin and she is naturally beautiful. The photos turned out nicer than our actual wedding photos in truth, and I became a bit frustrated that I'd found my love of the camera after our big day. Nevertheless, I had my portfolio.

I found that my dream of Soccer Saturday was all but gone. It wasn't what I was thinking about anymore. Now, I was thinking about Chesterfield sofas and photography.

With me holding the fort at the workshop and showroom, David was free to play the role of Business Development, and in early 2013, we hit the jackpot: Harrods. David had been spending a lot of time hanging around London's swanky spots, and we launched a second studio just off Sloane Square. This was just incredible for me. I hadn't visited London until I was 17 and hadn't been since, so it was a real eye-opener. David also rented an apartment not too far away in Fulham, and had it not been for just having Daisy and Lauren's midwifery training, I am pretty sure I would have been living in it myself. Nevertheless, I was more than happy to commute to support the new venture. After all, the people buying sofas on Sloane Square had a few more quid to play with, so this should be much easier than the back end of an industrial estate in Gateshead. I'd quite often jump on the 5:30 am train from Durham, commuting down to Kings Cross for 8:30 am, in the shop for 9:00 am, put my shift in, and then commute back on the 5:30 pm. I think back to it now and it seems a bit crazy, but I was just living off adrenaline. I was dreaming.

David and I had spent hours upon hours talking about London and what it would bring. He told me once that the first time we sold £100,000 worth of furniture in a calendar month, he would give me his Porsche. That was enough incentive for me to not want to go anywhere, not that I had any interest in going anywhere else. One evening, he took me to the Bvlgari Hotel in Knightsbridge. This was David's attempt at showing me what luxury really was, and how OSC would fit seamlessly into this kind of arena. He was right; the furniture would have fit in beautifully there. The bill came to about £250, and we only had a couple of small plates and a beer or two (I think David drank wine). When we were finished, he invited me to the cigar room. I didn't know what that meant really. I thought it was some kind of special meeting room or something like that. But no, when I walked in, I quickly realised that a cigar room is, in fact, a cigar room. A place where blokes go to buy and smoke expensive cigars. David asked me which one I'd like from the menu, so I did what all non-experienced cigar smokers would do. I chose the Cuban one. The waiter cut the end off and lit it up, and we found a seat next to an Arabian-looking guy and another man with an Eastern European accent. Where the heck am I? I thought to myself. The Arabian guy turned out to be a gold merchant, dealing in jewellery. The other guy, I don't know what he did, but he was negotiating, so I assume he was buying it. It was all very surreal.

A few months after we opened in Sloane Square, David set about launching in Harrods. He began speaking with them about the idea of putting some of our furniture into the famous department store, and they loved the idea. I was back in Gateshead when they came to visit. There were four of them, and they all looked immaculate, like they worked for Harrods, if that makes sense. It felt a bit like the day I saw David Moyes. I was so nervous; David and I knew this was a big deal.

When it was all signed and sealed, we had a lot of work to do. They were exceptionally demanding. We had around 12 pieces that we needed to make, mostly Manner One. Aside from this, we were contracted to a fixed sum for contributions to marketing. None of this mattered, of course, because once our furniture was in Harrods, alongside Sloane Square, the orders would come flooding in. I could smell the Porsche. We managed to get the pieces made and delivered to London and in place; it all looked incredible. They looked like £25,000+ sofas in there, and I was so excited.

The problem was, it didn't work. I have several theories about why. I think the investment was probably a lot more than we anticipated, and if I'm honest, we didn't prepare correctly in terms of recruitment. Of course, this wasn't my mistake, but I felt it all the same.

My biggest challenge at that time was dealing with customers. We'd have a call almost every day from a customer complaining, asking when their furniture would be ready. I'd fend them off for a bit, but eventually what you said last week either hadn't materialised or hadn't changed, and it was me starting to look incompetent. I didn't like that. It didn't sit well. As I said, I loved our customers, and it felt very personal when they turned on me. Having run a business myself now, I understand the predicament David was in. We had invested tens of thousands, if not hundreds, into both London sites, and sales just weren't coming as fast as we anticipated. The supply chain was becoming strangled as credit dried up, and thus orders weren't being made as quickly as they could be. There was discontent in the workshop, and I was trying to manage that, while also trying to keep customers and creditors at bay.

It was now 2014, springtime. I was worried. It didn't require a genius to recognise things weren't right. We weren't anywhere near that £100k Porsche month I'd been so excited about, and in truth, I was starting to get nervous about getting my wages, let alone a sports car. I was losing my mojo, and David knew it too - he had to have words with me a couple of times about my tone. The truth was, I was getting bored. One Saturday, I went into the workshop in the absence of any customers. I took a snip of leather and sewed it into a very rough, poorly-made phone case. I mixed a dye and I painted it. It was olive-coloured, with a splash of purple and walnut brown. I was quite pleased with my rough, poorly-made phone case. Lauren was too because she asked me to make her one. It soon became a bit of a thing I would do on a Saturday. I was being naughty, in truth, because I should have been innovating and coming up with solutions for our low sales, but I was simply out of ideas and if I'm honest, belief. I made a bookmark and a key ring. I was just pottering really. And then, out of nowhere, I had an idea. What if we could make shoes from this scrap leather? They'd be one-off shoes; one of a kind, like a Manner One sofa. Imagine what someone in London would pay for a one-off pair of handmade leather shoes. Imagine if I could do this; my business. Just imagine...

Chapter 5

Life on the Edge

I consider myself an incredibly positive person. I am the one who rescues others when they're in trouble with their mental health or personal troubles. I play down the small dramas in life, preferring to conquer the challenges and rise above the stress. Pressure is a good thing for me to some extent. It gives me energy. I am forthcoming when it comes to offering advice, delivering a rousing motivational speech on a football pitch, or captivating an audience with tales of resurrection and bouncing back from adversity. You will often find me connecting with people who suffer from shortages of confidence, willing them to look at things differently and open their minds to possibilities. When Lauren, my wife, was fed up with her job in hospitality, I marched myself down to the local college to find out what she needed to do to achieve her dream of being a midwife. Together, we conquered all hurdles; financial, emotional, and all those limiting beliefs. I knew she could do it, but Lauren didn't. That is how I love to spend my days, inspiring people and leading them towards greater outcomes for themselves.

I am very natural and very untrained, and that for me is why it works. I'm terrible at presenting because I'm incredibly scatty. It doesn't take long for me to digress from one topic to another, I drop a pen or forget where I am. That said, I don't get the impression people are often bored in my company or uninterested in my theories. In fact, quite the opposite. I often use the word 'running' when trying to articulate the inner feelings I get when I have my eyes on a prize and I'm gunning for it. I know that I am at my happiest when I'm running on adrenaline and wearing many different hats. I enjoy the feeling when I have that dreamy look in my eyes and I'm chasing it as hard as I can. When I have many topics to discuss and many theories to push, that's my happy place. In writing this book, I'm alive with happiness and excitement; I am running with it!

People often look at me and see an invincible human, a man of contentment, confidence, and self-belief. I receive a lot of praise and compliments for the things I've achieved and the paths I've taken throughout my career. I've had people tell me that they wish they had the courage to push themselves the way I do, something that I always push back on, reiterating my belief that nothing is impossible. This makes me proud because this is what I want people to think about me. I'm very privileged and humbled by those opinions.

However, the positivity I aim for in my daily life comes with a flaw. There's a flip side, which is often as intense as those days of invincibility. The lack of empathy and self-love that drove my behavioural problems as a child hasn't gone away. It's always there, and it doesn't take much for despair to kick in. These days can be incredibly tough for me to handle. In the same way that people often respond favourably to the positive side of my influence, people can get dragged into my low mood in equal measures, something no decent human wants to be guilty of. I don't like to be a negative person. I don't like to focus on fear or failure. I don't like accepting the word 'can't' or listening to excuses about the impossibilities that are in the way. I find it all incredibly frustrating, and I cannot stand it when the lows come. It makes me feel like I'm cheating myself; I find myself questioning my existence and which person is the true me. *Is it the depressive, low-mood, weak man who hates himself, or the confident leader striving for success?* When talking to Lauren when I'm in these depressive states, I often use the word 'fraud.' I'm a fraud. It's all a lie. I'm not the person everybody thinks I am. I'm blagging it. I'm cheating people into thinking I'm a positive person. I can lose sight of the dreamy man I take great pride in eulogising about. It's incredibly difficult.

As we know, mental health comes with so much stigma, particularly within men. As I sit here, in a positive state of mind, I am able to analyse and offer a balanced opinion on this. We associate the term 'mental health' with only the dark side. The term itself contains the word 'mental' which historically has been used as a negative adjective in describing one's state of mind. Depression, stress, anxiety, bipolar, psychosis, weakness, fear, grief. All words would connect with the dark side of mental health. But when you take a step back and consider the latter word, 'health', it makes a lot more sense to me. There is a positive side to the term. All mental health really means is the current state of your mind, and that doesn't have to be negative. Mental health isn't a bad thing. It's not an ugly thing to talk about. It's just the same as physical health. We can talk about a fracture or some tummy pains easily. We can talk about the wins in life, whether it's exercise, sport or love. If you can talk about all the good things in your life, excitement and joy, love and winning, awards and praise, then you can talk about the other side too. This philosophy is what makes it relatively easy for me to be so open. It's all mental health and you shouldn't shelter one side of it in lieu of the other. Being honest with yourself is where to start.

People have told me thousands of times that I'm brave to talk about my mental health, particularly the rough side of it all. People will have read the opening chapter of this book and considered it brave to share in the public domain my thoughts and feelings during the darkest and most vulnerable moment of my life. But ask yourself this; is it brave or is it something you can relate to? Most people know someone who has been where I have and so I suspect the answer is the latter, therefore going through tricky times like this can only be a normal thought process of a human being. I look at it very differently. If I'm brave, that implies that I have to be something to be able to be free of the stigma. To be able to talk and to be honest with people. I don't want to be brave, I just want it to be normal because making these conversations normal is what will ultimately save lives and improve outcomes for those requiring help. I want it to be common for people, men particularly, to open up about their emotions and thoughts, good and bad, and the things that are causing them difficulties. Life is not always good, there will always be tough things to deal with, so if it is normal that we talk about it, rather than pat someone on the back for being brave when they talk about it, then we will, without doubt, reduce suicide rates. Had it not been normal for me to be open about these things, I may not have sent Lauren that message to tell her I was beaten.

Being emotionally vulnerable is a wonderful thing. It's honest and pure. It delivers to you a release of the challenge you face and it delivers to others the opportunity to help. A problem halved, and all that. Nobody wants to be a sad sack or to revel in people feeling sorry for them. I certainly don't! But people will always help those who ask for it. It's quite simply human nature. And more so, people will always help those who are clearly helping themselves. This, for me, is often the first thing I look for when someone asks me to help them with a problem. What are you doing about it? How are you taking responsibility for yourself? Are you passing the blame? Are you making attempts to be healthier? This is even more frustrating for me when the same problem arises time and time again, and the individual is sitting on the same track without any attempts to get off the train. This is where mental health turns into self-pity, in my opinion. I understand this more than ever since I started running my own business, but this wasn't always the case.

As I reached my twenties, my seeking attention behaviour was showing no signs of letting up. I'd had a tough time in my late teens, living with my friend and his grandma after my dad and stepmam separated. Dad's mental health was out of control. He is a good example of someone who has stayed on the same track for most of his life, and the hardest thing to deal with is he is only too willing to ask for help, without helping himself. As a young man, I didn't have the capabilities to understand it, let alone deal with it. I was just angry. I was largely the victim of his problem, and I needed to get away. I'd fallen out with my stepmam, blaming her for a lot of the anger I felt as a young adult and for the way Rachel and I lived our teenage years. I met Lauren when I was just 17, in the midst of all the ill feelings and, in truth, I was a very confused individual. I said earlier it wasn't love at first sight and the reason for that was that I didn't feel like I knew what love was then. I didn't know what I wanted, other than for everyone to love me.

To make this happen, in order to get noticed, I created a caricature. Simon Bourne, a man who is different, quirky, and unique. It was entirely selfish and riddled with an ugly, insecure undertone. I sought attention, particularly that of girls, wherever I went. I'd spend time in online chatrooms, talking to girls as a way of fulfilling my desire to be loved. I'd go to parties and nights out with the intention of wandering off from my friends in order to meet new people and new girls. I'd engage in SMS exchanges well beyond what was appropriate for a man with a girlfriend; a man who loved his girlfriend. I was never content and found myself on more than one occasion begging for Lauren's forgiveness after being caught out. I never crossed the line physically, but I take no pride in knowing that. I understand now how my behaviour was not okay.

My insecurity developed into a smoke screen for my own actions, and as our relationship progressed through our twenties, my behaviour flipped into a darker, more controlling, manipulative, and jealous version of myself. I made Lauren's life very difficult, attempting to dictate her clothes, her friends, and her professional choices. I judged and questioned her about how or if she loved me enough. I was incredibly intense to live with.

I think most people look back at old photos of themselves and have an innocent giggle at their dress sense or questionable haircuts. I'm no different, although there is less innocence and more of a deep-cutting hatred. Not because of the image, which is funny, but because I don't recognise the man I see in old photographs or videos. He wasn't a nice person. I often delete old photos when they resurface on social media. While I still have an alternative dress sense and Lauren would tell you I certainly still carry questionable haircuts, the person I am today embraces these quirks as opposed to hiding behind them. The person I was back then certainly did not. My dress sense was awash with everything that nobody else wanted from the sale rail. I would create my own clothes by cutting them up or tarnishing them with bleach. I'd buy women's jeans because it was controversial. I'd dye my hair blue, purple, red, green, blonde, and black, and cut it into all manner of strange hybrid cuts. There was never a style, it was just a mash of confusion and expression geared towards one thing, seeking more attention and getting more reaction. It was, as I said, ugly.

Even journalism. I think my dream of Soccer Saturday and getting myself onto television was driven by insecurity. If I could get onto that show, my peers would remember me. I'd have some validation. They'd recognise me. They'd see me and they'd talk about me. I'd be noticed. My parents would see me on television, and I would be worthy of their affection.

My insecurity was a problem. I hated who I was. I didn't feel comfortable in my own skin. I felt like a failure. I thought I was a walking disaster and that I was impossible to love. My parents didn't like me. My siblings didn't like me. My teachers didn't like me. My girlfriend didn't like me. And so, wherever I went, I put on a show to try and get people to like me. If I dressed differently, I would be noticed. That's what drove every single buying decision on every item of clothing, and I carried it into all that I did and every action I took. I needed to make a song and a dance. I carried this hate for myself.

Of course, none of this was true. This was all my perception of myself. And I don't sit here writing as a preacher of recovery. Even today, Lauren has to check me on it every now and then and remind me to stop being so hard on myself. Likewise, I have to check myself when my desire to see my wife wear a particular outfit is either unfair or unkind. It hasn't gone away; I am not perfect. But I am aware of it and I know what is right and wrong.

Life for Simon Bourne before turning 30 was regularly wretched. Not because of what was going on around me, but because of what was going on within me. I'd spend a lot of time crying in secret, depressed and thinking about suicide. I'd overthink everything. I couldn't accept a kiss from

Lauren without analysing if she meant it, or if it was loving enough, soft enough, passionate enough, or if I was making it all up. I was carrying anger for those whom I blamed for it. My parents mainly. I had a vile and toxic temper. I would regularly visit the doctors, asking for counselling or medication without any real intention of changing. Visiting the doctor was just a way of excusing my behaviour. Truth be told, I didn't know I needed to change. I just thought this was who I was. My mental health was consistent in that it was inconsistent. One day I was okay, the next day I was in the rabbit hole of doom. I lived my life on the edge, and it was the duty of others to deal with it, or not. I am who I am; like it or lump it.

When Lauren eventually had enough of my behaviour and left me for a while in early 2009, I made all kinds of promises to her that I would change, but the reality was, that I wouldn't. I couldn't. I didn't know what the problem was. I thought it was everyone else; the ones who had let me down. I am not sure I would have been able to forgive Lauren if she had treated me the way I treated her during those times, but I'm grateful she did, and I can look back now, with my new mindset and recognise that she did so because she could see that there was far more in me than anger, temper, and ugliness.

I can pinpoint the turning point in life. It wasn't one thing, but a combination of events spread across a 2-3 year period. My trip to India, natural maturity, getting married, becoming a parent, but most of all, starting my business. When I started the business, everything changed for me. How I felt about myself changed. It had been coming, without me realising it, for a few years. The biggest impact was when I started working with David at OSC because of the relationships I built with customers. They liked me. They thought I was worth £15,000 of their hard-earned money. David and our customers all inspired me. I had the power to do that and it was entirely natural. That felt amazing. I felt worthy. David's attention and praise made me feel worthy. He rewarded me with extra pay and plenty of compliments about my ability and work. It mattered what I did, and that provided me with purpose. I started to like myself.

After I left OSC, I had a two-year stint with Sofa Workshop, a 'design your own sofa' high street retailer and part of the DFS group at the time. I was the manager of the Gateshead store, and my team of six all looked up to me as their leader. I thrived, but not just in that store, in the entire company. I made it my business to get involved in recruitment, training, marketing, and HR. I was never satisfied with simply running my store; I wanted to get involved with running the company. I felt I had a lot to bring to the table. My bosses respected me. Gateshead was a tough store to sell in, arguably the toughest in the company, and others before me had struggled to make it work. But, I did. We hit targets, we built a culture of going above and beyond. We won company awards for our service, and everyone in the company knew the name, Simon Bourne. I became somebody in those two years, and that felt amazing.

And then came Hand Dyed Shoe Co. My creation. My invention. My project. It was the final piece of the jigsaw really in terms of my self-healing journey. Almost overnight, it transformed my mindset and my personality. It gave me the ability to love myself. The self-destruction diminished, and I began to revel in who I was becoming. The person I became was integral to its success, so I began sharing my story publicly, realising that in doing so, I was building my profile and gaining more vindication and validation. I gained a plethora of fans, supporters, and customers for the business. People began asking me to speak at events and for my advice for their businesses. I realised I must be doing something right. I was useful after all. I was powerful. I might be more likeable than I originally thought.

The dark times never go away completely. I talked about pressure before. A little bit is exciting, but a lot of it is overwhelming. I still overthink things, particularly in difficult moments, but I am largely secure in my own skin and confident. It's not an act anymore. I analyse my decisions and my actions, but I try not to be too hard on myself either way. I recognise that all I can do is my best. The days just became less dramatic and less dark, I guess. That is what running a business did for me.

There's no doubt, that running a company is a very challenging and difficult task. But would I recommend it to people struggling with their mental health? Absolutely. Because of it, I am a better husband, a better parent, a better son, and sibling. I am more caring, more patient, and kinder. I am more responsible, more intelligent, and more rounded. I understand people better and I listen. I am braver in my opinions and more direct in my leadership. It helped me grow faster than anything else I had done before, and I am very proud of how Hand Dyed Shoe Co. built me into the man I am today.

Everybody on the planet has mental health challenges. I see all of the things that make up our mental health - or our personalities - as superpowers. The only difference between us is the severity of those challenges and our abilities to be able to manage them, whether that mental health is good or bad. It is undoubtedly about your mindset. You may have read this chapter and concluded that I perceive insecurity as a bad thing. I did, once. Today, I don't. I see it as the thing that pushed me into my journalistic achievements, something I am immensely proud of. My insecurities led me to Lauren and led me to fight for that relationship when things weren't easy. Insecurity led to me taking risks, leaving jobs where others would have remained, despite being desperately unhappy with their daily routines. This is using my insecurity superpower for good. Seeking the attention of women, anger towards my family, choosing clothes for other people's benefit, that's using my superpower for bad.

You can't look at any part of your personality and traits as a negative thing. Sharing your vulnerability is powerful. You are who you are and you think how you think. It's all part of you. Embrace it and don't put yourself under pressure to change who you are. Put pressure on yourself to accept who you are and then use what you know for the good of others and yourself. The bit you can control is how you express your quirks and how you use them to your advantage. The true rewards come when you accept yourself for who you are and stop bullying yourself for the seemingly ugly traits you bring to the party. You can use your superpowers for evil or for good. You choose.

Chapter 6

Get In The River

Soon after I had the idea for making shoes, I began researching shoemakers - or cordwainers as I learned they were formally called - all over the world, sending off what felt like a thousand emails. The idea was that we could use the scrap leather from the workshop, send the offcuts to the shoemaker, and they would craft the shoes before sending them back to us so that we could dye them. We could potentially create shoes worth thousands of pounds using little more than scrap leather. David would love it!

I found a local company called Bolton Bros. They specialised in orthotic shoemaking, and soon after I had sent my pitch email, I received a call from a guy called Tony Chisholm. He complimented me on the idea and said he thought it was brilliant. I was getting even more excited. I invited him down to the workshop to see what we were doing. I hadn't told David anything; I'd had this fantastical idea in my head that I wanted to get some shoes made, dye them, and then show him an example of my idea. That way, he couldn't say no. Tony arrived on Wednesday afternoon, and I gave him a tour of the workshop. He was very impressed. Tony was a professional in his industry, so his being impressed was a huge moment of encouragement. I felt like a businessman. He went into great detail, explaining the construction of shoes and what made Bolton Bros. so special. I didn't have the courage to tell him I didn't have a clue what he was talking about. Shoecraft was a world completely unknown to me. He asked me what kind of shoes I would like them to make. I didn't have a clue. I just said brogue - because that was the only type of shoe I knew of. I gave Tony some offcuts of leather, and he said he would take them back to the factory and be in touch.

A few weeks passed by, and I was beginning to think he wasn't going to get in touch. My impatience was crucifying me. I was desperate to tell Dave about my idea and to see his reaction. Tony called me just before lunch on a Friday while I was sitting at my desk. 'I have your shoes ready,' he said. I couldn't believe it. It was happening.

Tony arrived with a plastic bag in his hand. Out of the bag, he pulled out a pair of size 10 shoes. They were pearly white. The crust leather was raw. It was soft. It was the same feeling as the beautiful sofas we had on the trestles in our workshop. They were a work of art. Tony had some reservations about the leather, suggesting it was very difficult to work with due to its soft texture. Upholstery leather is often tumbled to loosen the fibres in the leather to give it more flexibility when stretched over a seat or arm. While that's brilliant for furniture, it's not ideal for a shoe that needs to be worn. It didn't put me off, though. I just figured we would have to find some way of reversing the tumbling technique to toughen the leather back up.

The shoes were a Derby style, as I was told. The good thing about a Derby is that they fit very comfortably due to the wings that fold over the top of your instep, apparently. I didn't care about any of that at that moment. All I wanted to do was get them in the workshop, mix up a dye, and get them painted. Tony left the shoes with me and said he'd be in touch with me the following week to see how David took the reveal. I didn't dye them straight away. I wanted David to see them in the raw form. I called him up and asked him to come to the studio. As was often the case, he was busy and couldn't get there that day, but he promised to come on Monday. It was a long weekend.

He arrived just before noon. He came in, wondering what all the commotion was about, assuming I'd sold an antique Chesterfield or something like that. 'I've got something to show you,' I said, trying to act cool in anticipation of his jubilant reaction. I had put them in a shoebox and wrapped them in tissue paper, which I'd specifically bought for the reveal. As I lifted the lid, there was a strong leathery scent that filled the room. A clever trick thanks to an air freshener I stashed in the bottom of the box. David lifted the snow-white shoe out of the box and rolled it in his hands like a rugby ball. He smiled, then lifted the shoe up and down as if testing the weight. 'Pretty cool,' he said. I went into my pitch.

'We throw away hundreds of bags of offcuts every year. It's perfectly good leather, just too small for a piece of furniture. Why don't we use it to make something else that can be hand-dyed, just like our Manner One sofas?' I wasn't sure what he was going to say, but the one thing I didn't expect him to say was no. 'There's no money in it,' he said. 'Berluti, Gaziano & Girling, Andrés Sendra. These boys have that market sewn up,' he continued.

I was devastated. I really thought he was going to love it, and that we'd set up a joint venture that we could work on alongside OSC. The idea was dead before it had even started.

When I got home, I told Lauren the news but I was far from defeated. Disappointed, yes. Devastated, yes. But I didn't agree that there was no money in a business like that. David was used to making large sums of profit on the sale of a luxury piece of furniture. It was a case of one sale per month could deliver enough profit to pay the overheads of the business and pocket him a tidy profit. The idea of plugging a shoe business into it that sold, let's say half a dozen pairs, but for a much smaller profit, didn't appeal to him. I understood. However, a small profit for me would be a fabulous business for me to run. There might not be millions in it, but perhaps there could be money in it for me if I pushed on.

I called Tony and broke the news to him that David wasn't impressed and the venture wasn't going to progress, but I followed up by telling him that I was interested in doing something myself. He was pleased; we'd struck up a relationship, and I think he was impressed by my lame impressions of a businessman. He said he was happy to work with me on the project. However, before we could progress, I needed to pay for the shoes they'd already made. It was a quick apprenticeship in the world of business. I had assumed he was making them as a sample, and they were free. We had never discussed prices - I thought it was all just experimental. £365 + VAT was the price.

SHIT!

I didn't have £365, let alone the VAT. I barely had a pound in the bank. I told Tony that I couldn't afford to pay that. He wasn't happy and came down to the workshop the next day to collect the shoes. Lesson learned, I guess.

Within a matter of a week, the business was dead, twice. First with David's rejection, and second when I lost my shoemaker because of the unaffordability of their labour. Again, I wasn't beaten. I just needed to find another shoemaker.

I spent hours on Google searching the globe for shoemakers and firing off emails. I had a couple of replies; one from China, another from Vietnam, and another from Pakistan, all willing to make single pairs of shoes in raw crust leather. Having learned my mistake, I asked them to confirm how much it would cost for a sample to be made. The costs to produce the samples were much better and more affordable, but I was put off by the broken English and the confusing methods of how I could pay. In the end, it was a factory in Spain that presented the best offering.

I'd chatted with Maria Boas, having found her contact information on a forum. She spoke great English and owned a shoe factory in the south of Spain. My research suggested Spanish shoemaking was of very high quality, and she knew exactly what I was looking for when it came to a raw crust leather shoe. The only problem I had this time was that she wanted a minimum order quantity of 50 pairs to produce the shoes. Each pair would cost me £130. That was £6,500.

The business was dead for a third time.

Maria and I chatted a lot over Skype calls, and I trusted her. She knew shoemaking far better than I did and she filled me with confidence. Lauren sat with me on one call so that I could get her opinion too. By the end of that call, we agreed that I should get a loan of £7,000 to fund the project. When I got the shoes, I'd then have 50 pairs which I could individually dye whatever colour the customer wished for, and I would make that £7,000 back easily.

I placed the order.

Almost overnight, things changed. Maria stopped replying to my emails and seemed to vanish. My stress levels went from fairly stressed to extremely stressed. I couldn't afford this loan and was relying on Maria to deliver these shoes.

Time went by, week by week, month by month. Maria was in contact, but it was vague, sporadic, and void of key information. With each response, I asked when I could expect to take delivery, questions which regularly went unanswered.

I threatened to contact the police, which seemed to trigger a response. I would have the shoes within four weeks, she told me. This was almost 20 weeks after I'd initially placed the order. Those four weeks passed, and still, there was no delivery.

Eventually, almost seven months after I placed the order, I received news that my 50 pairs of shoes were on the way. Only, when they arrived, there were only 36 pairs, and at least 20 pairs were completely unsellable due to the fact they had glue smeared on the surface of the leather, meaning it was impossible to dye them.

I never heard from Maria again.

It took a few weeks to come to terms with the scenario

I was now facing. I had £7,000 worth of debt, and I had no shoes of any significance to sell. It was a harsh lesson in business.

Lauren and I took a walk one evening to discuss what we were going to do. We took a few miles in, walking down the old railway line that used to serve the colliery. A few miles into our walk, we were making our way around a picnic area called Malton. Winding its way through the trees is a slow-running river called the River Browney. I'd spent a lot of time in my childhood plodging in the river and swinging from ropes over the deeper spots on a Tarzan swing. As we wound our way around a river bend, I saw a small sandy island emerge in the centre of the river. The water slowly ran either side of it, around a foot deep. When I think back to what I said in that moment, I get chills up my spine and the hairs on my arms stand up.

'Lauren, do you see that island in the middle of the river?' I blurted out.

'Yes,' she said.

'I'm going to carry my little table on that island, and I'm going to dye some shoes in the river.'

She looked at me like I was insane. 'Why?' she asked. I couldn't answer her with a more sophisticated answer than the one I gave her. 'Just, because,' was my answer. Seeking attention was probably the truth.

Lauren has gotten used to my bizarre ideas over the years. This was just another crazy haircut idea, and she knew that once I had it in my head, I would do it. A few days later, I drove to Malton with an old Victorian school desk in my car. I took my socks and shoes off and waded to the island. I placed the desk down and then ferried back and forth with everything I needed to dye the shoes. Members of the public could see me doing it and were taking photos of the strange man in the river sitting at a desk doing his homework. That's what it looked like. Lauren's brother Liam was a budding amateur photographer, so I asked him to climb in the river a little further upstream to capture the photo, which he did.

That strange moment changed everything.

A few days later, I posted the photo on social media. It was utterly bizarre. A few family members shared it, and out of the blue, I received an email from someone called Sarah Millington. I'd never heard of her, but she worked for the Northern Echo, arguably the biggest local newspaper in the North East. She'd seen the photo and wanted to know more about it. I told her all about my new business, The Hand Dyed Shoe Company. She asked if she could interview me for an article in the paper. I was chuffed. I'd never been in the newspaper before.

She came to my house and interviewed me, and within a couple of days, there it was, a full-page spread on page 13 of the Northern Echo.

'Get In The River,' has become a metaphor I use for getting out of your comfort zone. If you're nervous, worried, or doubtful, simply take a deep breath and *'Get In The River!'*

I didn't know it at the time, but getting in that river was the birth moment for my beautiful brand. A day or two after it was published, I received a message via my website from a man named Colin Elrick. He expressed an interest in what I was doing, told me he was getting married in a few months and would like to meet me to discuss getting some of my artisan shoes. I hardly knew what to say in truth. I'd become accustomed to selling sofas, but this was different. These were shoes. These were my shoes. I was out of my comfort zone.

I had little choice other than to blag it. I sent Colin my number, and he called me. I was petrified when I answered it. *What was he going to ask me? What if I didn't know the answer?* I didn't know anything about shoes. I didn't have a business plan; I just had 20 pairs of average-quality shoes. *What if I didn't have his size? What if they didn't fit or he didn't like them?* That would be embarrassing. Nevertheless, I answered.

Colin and I agreed to meet at Bannatyne's Café in Chester-le-Street on a Thursday around 10:00 am. It was my day off from OSC. As I walked in, I don't know why, but I knew who he was. He was well-dressed, wearing a nice blazer, dark denim jeans, and smart shoes. He told me they were a brand called Loakes. I wasn't familiar with it. The Officer's Club was more at my level. He explained he would often buy seconds from eBay or some guy in Newcastle selling factory rejects because they were a little cheaper than buying directly from Loakes. I don't think he told me that because he was a cheapskate; at this point, he didn't know how much my shoes were, and he was probably just pitching where he was in terms of his spending habits. I pulled out a couple of pairs of shoes, still in their raw leather, and I showed them to him. He mirrored David's initial performance when I showed him the sample, spinning the shoes through his hands, and turning them over to inspect the soles and the stitching. He asked if he could try one on, which of course I agreed. He said it was a good fit and felt good. I was encouraged.

Colin knew business. He was a big guy, and I got the impression he struggled with that, or perhaps had been struggling with that. He was vocal about some work he'd been doing on his image in the build-up to his wedding, working with a style coach and training at the gym to try and lose weight. He was a lovely man and clearly very in love with his fiancée. He told me he ran a business sourcing finance for other business owners and went into detail about it. Everything he said to me screamed that he was successful. He was a proper businessman. He told me of a friend of his, Jason

Knights, who ran a company called Blue Kangaroo, and how Jason was a multi-millionaire and would be very interested to hear about what I did. He suggested that he and Jason may well look to invest in Hand Dyed Shoe Company. That encouragement was enough to get me sweating in my chair. Maybe Jason could help me with my supply problems as well as my now debt problem.

We chatted for a good half an hour. Colin asked me if I'd like to join him at a networking event in Darlington. I said 'yes,' fearing if I said no, he might not buy my shoes. I didn't know what a networking event was. Eventually, attention returned to his wedding shoes. It was quick. 'Yes, I'll have a pair,' he said. 'How much are they?'

I hadn't thought about the price. I didn't know how to price them. There was the cost of making them, and my time to dye them. There was postage, the cost of time for the appointment with him. I stuttered, 'Let's call it £160,' I replied.

Colin was happy with that. In hindsight, it was a ridiculous price. I was making about £10 on the cost of the product for me to buy, but that excluded the several hours it would take me to dye them. However, rather like all those trips to Manchester and Old Trafford, I didn't care. This wasn't about money.

We shook hands, and I told him I would be in touch

within the next few weeks. We left the café, and I watched him climb into his brand new Mercedes while I opened the door with my key to a twelve-year-old, rusty Renault Scenic.

I called Lauren immediately. As soon as she answered, I burst into tears, overwhelmed by the achievement. It was a happy cry; I couldn't believe it. I had just sold a pair of shoes. This pair of shoes did not exist before I imagined them all those months earlier. This professional man, a businessman, had agreed to part with £160 of money on something I created. It was the best feeling outside of Daisy being born.

I felt worthy.

Chapter 7

Making a Shoe Guy

I spent £500 on an old gym floor and converted the small box bedroom in my house into a shoe dyeing workshop. Colin's shoes were the first pair I dyed for someone, and he was thrilled with the result. They accompanied him down the aisle on his wedding day, and, as I'm told, he felt a million dollars. That meant everything to me. Personally, as ever, I am my biggest critic, and I wasn't too happy with the finished product. Nothing specific, more just anxiety, second-guessing whether Colin would like them and deem them worthy of his £160. I'm thankful he did and he was proud to wear them.

I went along with Colin to the networking event, a 6.30 am start, before my shift. There was a complimentary bacon sandwich and freshly brewed coffee. Colin said I had to do a 30-second pitch in front of everyone. I didn't know about this until I got there. I hadn't rehearsed. I hadn't ever spoken in front of a large group of people before. I didn't know what to say. I just stood up, glared around the faces of the eagerly awaiting business folk staring me down awaiting some kind of wizardry, and then murmured for 30 seconds. I couldn't tell you what I said. When Colin stood, he introduced his business and then immediately began telling the room about me, his 'friend' the shoe artist. That's what he called me. I inhaled a quick breath and let out a shy smile. I'd never describe myself as shy, but I was at that moment. Almost embarrassed.

Over the next few months, I gradually sold a few more pairs of shoes. Andrew Morrison ordered a lovely derby style, and Jason Massingham, a local steel fabricator, bought a pair of whole cuts on the back of a 6.00 am meeting at his unit. John Haw, a man I'd never met, bought a pair after I posted on LinkedIn about my river story. Chris Adsett, another. Shoe sales gathered pace. The challenge was that I was getting to the bottom of my 20 pairs, and I hadn't factored into my price how to pay for the next batch of fifty pairs. The second challenge was that I didn't have a shoemaker to make them. It was all well and good being a Shoe Artist, but if you have no canvas to paint on, it'll be a pretty short-lived profession.

I can't exactly remember how I met Matteo Topponi, but his name alone said something about him. Italian. Italian leathers, Italian shoes. This man knew his stuff. I agreed to meet him in London. I wanted to show him some of my Spanish shoes and get his thoughts on them. He had been employed with some of the best shoemakers in the country, and he had a finesse for it. His father and brother, based back home in Perugia, were also shoemakers, so the prospect of working with this guy was good.

We met outside Harrods. Matteo was a small, diminutive man with that stereotypical Italian-defined goatee beard. He didn't come across much like a fashionista, like many of the Italians you see on TV, but he had his own style. As we made our way around Harrods, we talked about my previous dealings with them, and I showed him some of the furniture OSC had made that was still on display. As we made our way to the men's shoe department, my eyes really began to open. I picked up a Berluti shoe. The price tag was £2,950. Not far from Berluti, there was Louis Vuitton. A black pair of whole cuts made in real crocodile skins. £6,500. I don't know why I was surprised, but it just blew my mind. The Officer's Club couldn't be more different. The whole event took me back to the cigar room. I imagined the Arab guy parading around Harrods, trying on Berluti shoes and purchasing them without a second thought on how he might pay his energy bills next week. Matteo looked at them differently from me. He looked at them for their construction and quality. He was pointing out flaws; I couldn't see any. But it was enough for me to know I'd like to work with this guy.

When I returned to Durham later that evening, I wrote to him and asked if he would consider making shoes for me. I asked him what his minimum order quantity might be and what prices he would charge. I asked him how long it would take him to make them, about whether his shoes would have any glue on them. He said he would have a think and would come back to me.

A short while passed, and I was getting anxious. I needed some more shoes pretty quickly. Matteo wrote and said that he didn't think he could make it worth his while because he had just secured a contract with Gaziano & Girling in Northampton and he needed to focus on that. However, he said that his brother Lorenzo, over in Perugia, would be willing to help.

I quickly rebuilt my website, eulogising about our new Italian shoes. I bought stock images of Italian-looking shoemakers, old men in quintessential pokey little workshops making shoes. I needed to create a brand and sell the story of Lorenzo and Matteo. Lorenzo came back and said he would make 25 pairs at a time. Perfect, I thought. It was only £3,500 I had to find. By this point, Lauren knew how invested I was in it all, and she put up little argument. We could get another loan, and we did. This time, I paid Lorenzo 50%. I didn't have time to wait for samples, so I gambled, assuming that based on what Matteo had told me and how well he talked about quality, they would be beautiful.

Two weeks. That was the commitment from Lorenzo, and he didn't let me down. To his credit, all 25 pairs arrived ahead of schedule. Sadly, however, all 25 pairs were no good. This time, it was the leather. It was too soft. I don't actually know what it was. It felt almost like suede, with a furry texture. I barely had the heart to tell Lauren. I was in it up to my eyes now.

I think I sold one pair of Lorenzo's shoes to an old colleague of mine, Paul McGinnety, who reached out and offered some support. He never came back for any more, and it didn't surprise me. I was more than embarrassed to send him the shoes, to be truthful. I knew they weren't right. To this day, I still have 24 pairs of Lorenzo's shoes. More memorabilia.

The business was dead, again. Only this time, I had a big loan to repay too.

I was struggling. The guilt. The regret. The failure. The debt. It was so hard. I was lucky that things were progressing quite well with Sofa Workshop, and my salary had increased a good few hundred pounds a month from when I was working with David. It was just enough to cover the loan repayments, but I knew it was going to be a long five years ahead.

I was at work one day when I received a message via email from a guy called Rui. It was broken English, so I knew he wasn't in the UK. He told me he could help me with shoemaking and that I should contact him with any requirements

I have. I had no money, and I certainly had little interest in getting any more credit, so I ignored it. He emailed again. 'Mr Simon,' he would call me. I replied and told him that the Hand Dyed Shoe Co. was closing unless he could make me some samples and send them to me, for free. I didn't expect him to reply, but he did. He asked me some more questions about what I was looking for. 'Raw crust leathers, handmade shoes,' I told him, 'minimum order quantity of one.' I knew without money or more credit, I was not able to commit to more than that. I told him what I needed in terms of lead time and price. I didn't expect a reply, but he did.

Mr Simon,

Here in Portugal we have many factories. We beautiful make shoes. We help you. Please await samples.

Your friend,

Rui.

The samples arrived, and they were stunning. More beautiful than the Spanish shoes. More beautiful than the Italian shoes. They were amazing. The leather was soft and supple. It wasn't furry. The stitching was faultless. I reviewed them using all the pointers Matteo had told me to look out for. They were immaculate. This was the first time I had a product I really believed in. And yet, for the first time in my professional life, I stalled. I took a step back and stopped running. I stopped dreaming. This is too good to be true, I thought. This can't go on. I've spent too much, we're in too much debt to go again. I couldn't put Lauren and Daisy through this anymore.

I emailed Rui again, thanking him for the samples and giving him a glowing review. I told him I needed some time to think. He replied, inviting me to Portugal to meet him and his friend Silvia. . .

Fuck!

I logged into my online banking account. We had about £200 in the bank. We had no savings or anyone we could turn to for a sub. I thought and thought about how I could sell this to Lauren. I needed to go to Portugal. I needed to know what Rui could do.

I got home and prepared all my research. I knew the following week, my shifts at Sofa Workshop landed so I had Monday and Tuesday off work. I looked at flights online and found that I could get a flight from Liverpool to Porto for £29 on Monday at 1.00 pm. I could fly back to Edinburgh on Tuesday at 8.30 pm for the same price. I'd need accommodation in Portugal, but I could find a hostel for about £20. The train to Liverpool would be £60, and the train back to Durham from Edinburgh would be £40. The problem was that I wouldn't land in Scotland until after the last train back to Durham had left, meaning I had a problem getting to my shift for Wednesday. If Rui would collect me from the airport, I wouldn't need a hire car. If I slept in the Edinburgh airport, I wouldn't need a hotel when I got back. I concluded that it would cost £178 to go to Portugal. All I needed to do was come up with an excuse for not being available in my store that Wednesday.

I was fortunate that my reputation at Sofa Workshop was pretty solid, and I was known for helping other stores out when there was a shortfall in education or skill. I called my boss and explained that I felt our new manager in our Edinburgh store could use a little bit of help with the systems, etc., and I kindly volunteered my services. They agreed that I should go up there on Wednesday to assist him. Bingo.

I'd grab the train Monday morning, fly to Portugal from Liverpool, find my hostel, and meet Rui. We'd meet again Tuesday morning to talk business. I'd then fly back to Edinburgh, and make myself comfortable on a bench - people would just assume I'm waiting for a flight. In the morning, I'll grab a bus to our Edinburgh store to meet Mark. I'd spend the day there and then travel back. And what's more, I'd get Sofa Workshop to pay for my train back on expenses.

I had it all planned out. It was all arranged with work

and Rui. I had all the tabs open on my laptop ready to book what I needed. Now all I needed to do was convince Lauren.

We sat down. She'd already seen the samples and was in agreement they were excellent. I told her Rui had invited me to Portugal. Her response, as expected, was 'Well, we can't afford that.' She was right. We couldn't. Beyond that, she was protecting me because she knew I had been through the wringer with guilt and failure. She didn't want me to be disappointed anymore. Eventually, again, she gave in to my convincing argument that I should do this and she agreed that I should explore this one last time.

Monday came. I arrived in Portugal on time and met Rui at the airport. I was right; he spoke almost zero English at all. He was a dwarf, something I obviously hadn't imagined. I jumped in his car, and he took me to his office, about a 30-minute drive from the airport in Aveiro. When we arrived, he introduced me to Silvia. Silvia was a beautiful lady; she spoke almost perfect English and made me feel very welcome. I told her all about my exploits with Maria and Lorenzo and where I felt it had gone wrong. She reassured me that she and Rui would find a solution to my challenges. I don't know if this was to set me up or not, but almost with her final point of reassurance, she pulled out a contract and placed it in front of me. I was taken aback. A contract, that's like... legal, right? I couldn't sign a contract. *What would that mean? What would Lauren say if I told her I had signed a contract with some Portuguese duo whom I'd met barely an hour earlier? Stuff it.* I did it anyway. I signed it. I wasn't even sure what it was, but I signed it.

I boarded the 8.30 pm flight back to Edinburgh. I was so excited. I'd done it. This was it. I trusted Fatima instantly. I trusted Silvia. I had a supply chain that had no limits. I had a supply chain that I had pure belief in. I knew Fatima wasn't going to let me down.

When I landed back in Edinburgh, it was late. I settled in at the airport, knowing I had a long night ahead of me. I couldn't wait to get back to Lauren and Daisy to share the incredible news.

Over the next few months, I worked closely with Fatima and the factory in Portugal. They produced samples that were even better than I could have hoped for. The shoes were stunning, and I knew they would be a hit with customers. I started promoting them on my website and social media, and the response was overwhelmingly positive. Orders began to come in, and for the first time, I felt like I was on the right path with my business.

I continued to work my day job at Sofa Workshop to support my family and repay the loans we had taken out to fund the business. It was a challenging and exhausting juggling act, but I was determined to make it work.

As the Hand Dyed Shoe Co. grew, I started to gain

recognition in the industry. I was invited to attend events and network with other professionals. I even had the opportunity to collaborate with a well-known fashion brand on a limited-edition collection of hand-dyed shoes.

The business wasn't without its ups and downs, but I had learned valuable lessons from my past mistakes. I was more cautious with my finances, and I focused on building a strong and reliable supply chain. Most importantly, I believed in the quality of my product and the brand I was creating.

Looking back on my journey, I realised that getting in the river that day to dye shoes had been a pivotal moment. It led me to meet the right people, find the right suppliers, and ultimately build a successful business. It was a reminder that sometimes, taking risks and stepping out of your comfort zone can lead to incredible opportunities.

I knew that there would still be challenges ahead, but I was ready to face them head-on. I had Fatima on my side and I knew she wouldn't let me down. With determination, hard work, and a little bit of luck, I was confident that the Hand Dyed Shoe Co. would continue to thrive and grow, providing beautiful, handcrafted shoes to customers around the world.

Chapter 8

Tipping Point

My two years with Sofa Workshop were arguably the best use of my time in my entire career to date. Yet, when I accepted the job, it was the last thing I wanted to do. All I wanted was to change the way the world buys shoes.

When they offered me the job, it wasn't a cause for celebration; I had mixed emotions. On one hand, it was a terrific opportunity to work in what I felt was a growing company with a fabulous history and a very creative day-to-day sales role. Sofa Workshop was essentially a design-your-own-sofa company, and most of my days were filled with helping people create their dream pieces of furniture. It involved interiors, design, art, and sales. They were even offering me a role as the designated manager of their brand-new North East store—a trainee manager, for lack of a better description. It was a role that didn't exist when I applied, one they were willing to create to get me on board. It was flattering, to say the least. On the other hand, I had to leave David. I had to walk away from the promise of a Porsche and everything we'd been working towards. I had to leave the trips to London and the flashy cigars with the gold dealers. OSC was my baby. I was that invested. Leaving for another sofa retailer felt harsh. And then, there were the shoes! I wanted to do this more than anything else. I wanted to work for myself and be my own boss. I wanted to be the master of my destiny. I didn't want to ask for days off or holidays any more; I wanted to decide for myself when I would be at work or not. It was, without a doubt, one of the toughest decisions I've ever had to make in my life. I spoke to most of the people close to me, particularly my friend Mary, who was often the voice of reason in my world. I even wrote a three-page letter explaining the pros and cons of each decision and passed it around to people to help me decide what to do. The problem with that was that you get those who think left and those who think right. The lefts would generally say, 'Follow your dreams, go do the shoes,' but I knew that it wasn't ready to support us financially. At this point, it was still merely a hobby, if that. The rights would usually bring it down to money and security. They'd suggest playing David and Sofa Workshop off against each other to try and negotiate a bigger pay packet or opportunity. Lauren was mostly concerned about how comfortable I had it with David and what I might be walking away from. I was kind of my own boss anyway, and I had plenty of time on my hands to do things I wanted to do while waiting for a customer to come in. I wouldn't get that in a bigger, more corporate company. I'd be expected to work harder, and I would have to work most weekends. That didn't sit too well with me; weekends would soon become more precious once Daisy started school. I'd never felt more confused.

I met David for a coffee at Newcastle Train Station. My heart was beating faster than the Edinburgh to London service speeding through the middle track. I was deeply anxious. I'd decided I was going to tell him about Sofa Workshop and their offer. I wasn't putting a decision on the table; I just wanted to see what he thought. In truth, I was hoping he would convince me to stay. I wanted him to do that; to put a deal on the table that made it impossible for me to leave. Maybe even offer me that Porsche. But in reality, I knew he couldn't because I knew OSC was struggling. It was, for want of a kinder phrase, a sinking ship.

He took it well, although he was shocked. I don't think he saw it coming, but David is a gentleman of very little external emotion. He remained humble, where others might have let their damaged ego and disappointment lead the conversation. I learned a lot from him in this moment, arguably the most powerful lesson I had under his stewardship. Remaining humble while everything inside you screams alternative thoughts is a skill that not many people have when they're under pressure - which I knew David was. It's a very hard thing to do when you're shocked, but David is the best I've ever seen when it comes to handling pressure; at least on the outside. We sat for a few hours talking about it all. We talked about London and how it was 'on the cusp,' which was one of his favourite phrases. I've inherited it since, to be fair. We talked about Harrods and the opportunities that we had there if we could just get it working for us. We talked about Sofa Workshop and what they were offering, and David suggested we could do something a bit different. He mentioned that he could do a deal with some equity in the business, which, given how emotionally invested I was, felt very exciting. Maybe a little pay raise too, he suggested. I could move into his Chelsea apartment in London and run our Sloane Square store. There were options, so we ended our chat with a gentlemanly handshake before I headed back to work.

It was a long 24 hours waiting to see what kind of deal he would come up with. The anxiety I felt the day before had turned to anticipation and impatience. He called me shortly after lunch. I let it ring a few times; I didn't want him to think I was sitting, staring at my phone waiting for it - which I was. In my head, I was playing this now; I was being a professional businessman, looking to strike a deal to benefit myself and my family. I answered it with authority. But David seemed coy. After the obligatory, 'How are you feeling?' we got down to it.

'Simon,' he said, 'I think you should take the job with Sofa Workshop.'

I was gutted.

I was not expecting that at all. Even though I knew OSC was struggling, I just didn't expect him to say that. What came next was, in my opinion, a true testament to him and his character.

'Simon, you have a young family. Their offer is very good. You'll develop there. It's a good deal for you; you should take it,' he courteously explained.

He was right. I just didn't want to hear it. I was devastated it was over. I was scared that I might not be able to adapt to corporate work and the more cut-throat nature of furniture sales. *What if I got sacked after a week? What would I do with my private registration plate?* What a stupid decision it was to buy that. I had so many thoughts going through my head, but he was right.

I wrote an email almost immediately to Sofa Workshop's HR department. That in itself felt weird - OSC was a team of 5 people; I was the HR department. I accepted the post of designated manager and looked forward to joining them.

A few weeks later, I was invited to Harrogate to meet the store manager and experience Sofa Workshop as a mystery shopper. It was love at first sight. Not only did I love the sofas, but I also loved the brand and the experience. Lauren and I co-created a stunning Caruso three-seater sofa with three deep-filled feather and down cushions, and a coil-sprung seat, delightfully upholstered in a grey washable linen. It was amazing; I just loved how collaborative it was. I didn't feel like I was being sold to at all, which was something I was worried about. I thought they would be expecting some kind of robotic, game-playing used car salesman tactics from me - something I knew nothing about at all - but this wasn't like that at all.

I started the job in their Glasgow store and sold a Dillon three-seater sofa on my first day. What a feeling that was. Glasgow was a new store, like the Gateshead store where I was due to be positioned. In Glasgow, we had a team knitted together featuring experienced Sofa Workshop legends Liz and Will - the top salespeople in the company. We had Arnoldas, Sam and Olly, three up-and-coming reputable sales guys. Then there was Mary, a typical Glaswegian new to the job but you couldn't tell. For some, it would have been quite an overwhelming force to slot into, but I didn't feel like that at all. I felt welcome and as though I'd been part of the company for as long as Liz and Will had. I instantly bonded with them all, and given that I was off the mark with the sales pretty much straight away, I think that earned me a few bonus points too.

I stayed in Glasgow for 4 to 5 weeks. I enjoyed it, but I was looking forward to getting to Gateshead, which was due to open soon. My role as designate manager meant that my duty would include covering stores within the company when managers had annual leave, but in truth, that was never a role I wanted. That meant long periods away from Lauren and Daisy. I wanted the job of manager at Gateshead, but it had already been offered to a chap called Mark before I interviewed. Otherwise, I think I would have been offered it. Once we started, I just focused on my numbers. Gateshead was a tough gig to sell in. We were the only store-in-store model within the Sofa Workshop network; we shared a floor with DFS, who had recently acquired Sofa Workshop just before I started with the company. It meant, in essence, that while we were the same company, we were rivals, and that made it difficult because the DFS salespeople would do everything they could to disrupt our progress.

Nevertheless, I hit the ground running. Week after week, I was at the top of our team when it came to sales. I was loving it. My name was reverberating around the company. I was even challenging Will, who ran the top-performing store in Exeter, a much more affluent part of the country than Gateshead. Yet, here I was competing. I quickly learned that my style was very natural, and that's what made it work so well. Authenticity was the key. I could connect with a customer very quickly, whether they were a wealthy, political, art-enthused architect or a rough-and-ready single mam from a run-down area of Newcastle; I could strike a relationship with little more than an opening hello. That was my gift.

The store didn't get off to the best of starts, and I think Mark was intimidated by my presence, in truth. I tried not to intimidate him because I genuinely wanted to support him, but it was quickly apparent that the team was responding more to my leadership qualities than to his. He was commuting a lot from Doncaster, where he lived, up to Gateshead while he worked it all out; it was quite a commute, and I think that, along with my presence, led him to step aside from the role as manager around six months after I'd started. I would be lying if I said I was sad about it. I wasn't. I was very excited about what I could do here.

We were operating as a team of six. I became the store manager, with 5 sales staff in my team. I focused my leadership on three areas: numbers, accountability, and, most importantly, fun. One of the first things I did was create a dashboard, an Excel spreadsheet that would give everyone their key statistics, including revenue, number of units, and additional insurance policies sold. It covered everything that could be measured. I felt it was imperative that if we were given a target as a store, it needed to be distributed among us all on a weekly basis. If you hit your target but other team members missed it, there was accountability. One member of the team could not let their standards slip much beyond a week or two because it was glaringly obvious. Without a doubt, this dashboard was the greatest tool I could have created to drive in-store competition and manage accountability.

Without a doubt, though, the most important area I focused on was fun. We had the numbers and we had targets, but I wanted to put Gateshead on the map for camaraderie and fun, for togetherness and friendship. We had each other's backs. I wanted everyone in the company to be talking about us for far more than just numbers. I wanted Gateshead to be an environment that my team enjoyed because if I could create that, if I could take that small part of my personality and influence my team to do the same, our customers would feel it too.

I couldn't have explained that at the time - I wasn't entirely aware that this was what I was doing - it's only now when I reflect that I can understand that my leadership was just an extension of who I am as a person and the things that make me tick.

In the winter of 2016, I attended a managers' meeting in London. It was a celebratory evening as Gateshead was awarded two trophies in our annual presentation. The first was for the Top Net Promoter Score (NPS) within the company, which meant a lot because NPS is a scale where customers who have purchased from your store rate your service levels. We had the highest score in the company.

The second award was one I was most proud of. It was a special award that had previously not been given, the 'Above and Beyond' award. It was created to highlight a specific piece of work that our leadership deemed above and beyond the norm. The reason I was most proud of this was because, for me, there was nothing above and beyond about it. The piece of work it related to was nothing more than Gateshead just being Gateshead.

We had a great team, and everyone in it bought into what we were doing. We all had our disagreements at times, but it was never more than that. I had recruited a young guy named Liam Silcock who joined us from a business that sold window blinds. He was an infectious character, very much a rough diamond, but I felt he had potential backed by his instant likeability.

One day, a customer came into the store on a quiet Sunday afternoon looking for a sofa bed, and she needed it quickly because she had family arriving the following Wednesday. Our furniture typically took 8-10 weeks to craft, so new wasn't an option. We checked our stock system to find that we had one, an ex-display piece in our Derbyshire warehouse. Delighted, the customer placed an order for it.

Monday arrived, and we called the warehouse to inform them that we had sold the sofa bed they had. It was there, in good condition and ready to deliver. The problem was, they weren't going to be in the North East until Thursday. With the customer's family due to arrive on Wednesday, our only option was to refund the customer and wish her well in her search. I guess that would be considered the 'norm.' I had instilled a philosophy in the team that naturally encouraged them to think outside the box. I would often say that those inside the box would only ever achieve what the box allows them to achieve. If you get outside of it, you quickly learn that the possibilities are endless. You just need to *'get in the river.'*

We called every local courier we could find and asked them for a quote to pick up the sofa bed and deliver it before Wednesday. Not many were able to do the job at such short notice, and those who agreed to do it priced themselves out. Liam and I hatched a plan: we could hire a van from a local depot. The drive to the warehouse would be around two-and-a-half hours and the same back. Since we were both scheduled to work on Tuesday, we knew we couldn't get to the warehouse in time before it closed at 5.00 pm. That left us with one remaining option.

We collected the van that Tuesday afternoon went home, had dinner with our families, and got some rest. We met in a car park just south of Durham at 4.00 am and set off on the two-and-a-half-hour journey. We arrived as the first warehouse staff pulled into the car park alongside us. We loaded the sofa bed, drove back to Newcastle, and delivered it before noon, just in time for the customer's family arriving at 1.30 pm.

It's an ethos that has never left me, nor Liam, who has gone on to have a successful career in the sales industry. The Above and Beyond Award was a very proud and humbling moment, but I think the beauty of the lesson was that, for me, nothing about it was going above and beyond. My job, first and foremost, was to sell furniture. Without doing that, I would have had to refund the furniture, and that thought alone didn't sit well with me, let alone the disappointment the customer would have inevitably felt. I had built a culture that explored every option to make a sale and, even more so, to keep one.

Overall, I spent two and a half years with Sofa Workshop. I don't believe that my shoe idea would have lasted much more than a few weeks had I not served that time with the company. Going from a small business like the Original Sofa Company, whose ambition of a one-million-pound annual turnover felt sizable, to a company employing 250 people, a supply chain, a marketing team, HR, and a finance department, with over 25 stores nationwide. I needed that education, even if I perhaps didn't want it.

Outside of work, my shoe business was beginning to take shape. My employers knew about it, and they didn't object to me doing it. I think, to be honest, by the time they found out, they were quite willing to turn a blind eye to it based on the fact my store was doing well. I'd built a website and developed a business model that enabled me to visit clients to help design their unique pair of handmade shoes. I didn't have premises, so I innovated, using cafés, bars, or hotels to meet clients and talk them through the process. I even met one guy in a car park off the motorway, which most definitely caught the attention of a few passers-by as I stood on the floor having measured his feet - and not for the right reasons! All my meetings were arranged outside of work hours. It was a lot, running this micro-operation on top of my 40–50-hour job, but it didn't matter. I was never tired; I just did it. I once met a great entrepreneur named Jason Massingham at 6.00 am at his steel fabrication yard. I helped him create his unique shoes and was then in my office by 8.45 am, with nobody any the wiser that I'd been anywhere else that morning. My work ethic and motivation were incredibly high for both aspects of my life: my job and my budding business.

I had always aspired to go it alone one day, but the reality was I really enjoyed my job with Sofa Workshop, and therefore, I never felt like it was in the way of my ambition. My tipping point, when it came, was probably more obvious to my bosses than it was to me.

I had taken the Gateshead store as far as I could. There wasn't much more I could achieve there, and I was yearning to try something new. Lauren and Daisy were very settled in the North East, so the idea of relocating was never an option. There weren't any other stores in the North that I felt would be a step up. I could have pushed myself into a more regional role, supporting all the stores in the North, but the commuting didn't appeal to me. I dabbled with a training and development role for a while, stepping into a new arena designed to inspire and educate new recruits to the company. I enjoyed it, to a point. Perhaps I would have enjoyed it more if my shoe business weren't selling so well in the background.

By October 2017, I'd had a couple of disagreements with my boss who had accused me of becoming distracted. I didn't like that because I had a lot of love for Sofa Workshop and my team. I felt it questioned my integrity and credibility in the job. She felt that it was my ego that was hurt. My honest opinion is that if there was a role in Sofa Workshop I could have transitioned into, I would have stayed longer and would have been content to keep my shoe business as a side hustle. But there wasn't, and so I started to think about it in bigger, more exciting, and creative ways.

By November, I signed a deal with a local businessman to rent a small unit where my customers could come to see me, rather than me travelling to see them. The Clydesdale Suite in The Courtyard of Langley Park was about the size of a single garage. That day, for me, was the day the business truly began. It was now a real business.

Chapter 9

Living The Dream

I worked my final day of employment on 9th December 2017. By this point, as my boss had told me on a few occasions, I had checked out. I didn't have much interest in Sofa Workshop anymore. The company had undergone a restructure, and I didn't feel like it was going in the right direction. Most of what was beautiful about the company was now diluted into little more than statistics and sales. When I first joined the business, I immediately felt a sense of love for what the people who represented it felt for the brand. At the centre of the business were creative characters who had been there, in some cases, for decades, and that core was almost all but gone by the time I left. I always felt it was the wrong approach. The new CEO came to meet me in Gateshead, and I tried to explain where I felt the company was going wrong and how, if I were her, I would focus on retaining and reinstalling some of the passion that had been lost. I followed this up with a detailed analysis of the business and what I felt were glaringly obvious failings, poor leadership qualities, and corporate decision-making. She didn't last long in the job after I left, thus I conclude it all fell on deaf ears. What was left of the nucleus beyond my departure soon followed, and as such, a few years later, the company collapsed altogether. I felt a deep sense of sadness because even today, I still say that Sofa Workshop was the greatest place on the planet to buy furniture.

Without a doubt, going self-employed was a bizarre feeling. I remember waking up on day one of not having a job and thinking about how weird it was. I was the master of my destiny. I know for certain that there were people close to me, even at that moment, who disapproved of my decision to leave what they perceived as a secure, well-paid job. I had a young daughter and a mortgage. I had no evidence that this company could pay me anywhere near the salary I was getting at Sofa Workshop. I didn't even have a business plan. And they were right; all those things were true, but I knew that without the shackles of employment and the monotony of a rota dictating my movements, I was free.

Employment for me always felt a little bit stressful. My mental health was regularly up and down with the highs and the lows of day-to-day life. I was, after all, too emotional. And so it seems crazy to think that self-employment and the up-and-down nature of business might serve me better, but it did.

Lauren and I had agreed that we would try it. We never

agreed on a time scale or a minimum amount that I had to sell to keep going; we just agreed that we would try. Even today, as I write this story, I'm not sure we've ever concluded what the trial is or if it has been a success or a failure. We're still just trying.

I welcomed my first-ever customer to my new studio on 13th December 2017. He bought a pair of Mr Rump brogues - an Oxford, he told me. It was my first wake-up call when it came to learning on the job. I didn't know what an Oxford was at that moment - only that it was a style of shoe. I Googled it as soon as he left and taught myself the differences between Oxfords, Derbys, and various other styles.

Those first few weeks were crazy. Christmas was upon us, and one of my first observations was that I no longer had a team to have our annual Christmas night out with. But, I was free, so I called my mate Jack, and we booked four nights in Barcelona. The Hand Dyed Shoe Co. Christmas night out. It was a tricky one to sell to Lauren, I won't lie. I'd just quit my job. We had no idea if or when I would next receive a salary. But I felt pretty wealthy at the time - I'd been working full time, earning good money with Sofa Workshop, while selling half a dozen pairs of shoes per week on the side - so I felt like I could burn a few quid.

Barcelona was great. It was an insight into what I felt self-employment would be like for years to come: beaches, money, freedom, travel, and parties. I was the richest man on the planet those few days.

As Christmas came and went, moving into 2018, I was beginning to get more nervous about how long I could string this out. We decided that we needed to get hold of the numbers. Lauren and I went to the local retail park and bought a whiteboard. We worked out how many pairs of shoes I needed to sell to pay myself the same salary I was getting at Sofa Workshop. The number was somewhere between 20-22. But, in order to sell that many, we needed to do some marketing - exhibitions, social media adverts, things like that. I'd read somewhere online that your marketing spend should be 25% of your profit. So, that took it to around 25-30 pairs. It was another wake-up call. We were doing around 15 pairs, on average, at this moment. I was a little more nervous now.

A few days passed by when the moment hit me. We'd been watching Dragons' Den for years on the BBC. It didn't really have much to do with my interest in business. It was just light television on a Sunday night as much as anything. I'd always watch, and Lauren and I would dissect the pitch, like most viewers. And I'd often follow that up by declaring how I'd love to have a go.

That was a very exciting idea for me. If I could get on Dragons' Den; what if I could get an investment? Even if I didn't get one, I'd get so much exposure from it that it would put the brand on the map, so to speak. I told Lauren. She laughed; as she does. She knew I was mad. But that was fuel to me; the perfect fuel. I searched for an application form and completed it immediately. I sent it in, sat back, and waited. I waited. And I waited. I waited for weeks and heard nothing. I was naturally disappointed. By this point, I was searching for the producers on LinkedIn and Facebook, trying to see if I could find any clues as to how best to approach them. I considered driving down to Manchester where the BBC studios were and walk in with some beautiful shoes on my feet.

I was in the studio when the email eventually came. It was a personalised email - which straight away encouraged me because it wasn't generic. It read:

Hi Simon,

Thank you for your application for Dragons' Den. Your application was fantastic.

Unfortunately, applications for series 17 are now closed but we would like to keep your company in mind for series 18 which we will be filming next year.

Best regards,

Veronica.

I had a whirlwind of emotions when I learned that the producers at Dragons' Den were interested in my business, although I was disheartened to realise it would be at least a year before they'd consider my application further. Nevertheless, this experience instilled a sense of belief in me. If I could pitch my business to the Dragons, the Ashley Ficklings of television, I could conquer any challenge that came my way. The key was to persevere, and so that's exactly what I did.

During my tenure at Sofa Workshop, I had the pleasure of meeting Ann English, a local entrepreneur whose business helped people to visualise. She and I first crossed paths in an urban café in Gateshead one evening after I had completed a long 12-hour shift at the furniture store. After wrapping up my work, I immediately switched gears to talk about shoes. Ann's business, Create Intrigue, was essentially a business management consultancy, specialising in creative problem-solving and innovative solutions. She was an expert in visual communication and served as a coach.

Over coffee, I confided in Ann about the chaotic jumble of thoughts swirling around in my head. I struggled to organise them into any coherent plan or structure. My ultimate goal was clear: to build a multi-million-pound business that would grant my family and me financial freedom and the ability to make choices not dictated by our past. This vision was a far cry from my upbringing as a boy from Scunthorpe, seemingly destined for a very different path, one that led to fighting, prison or drugs. I felt like I wasn't meant to have a thriving multi-million-pound company or the finer things in life.

Ann proposed an intriguing idea - we should have a session where I would talk, and she would document my words. From there, she would create a Vision Tree encompassing everything that flowed from my mouth. It sounded like a wonderful concept.

In early 2018, I booked the session, which came with a price tag of £195. It turned out to be one of the best investments I ever made in myself. We spent over four hours delving deep into various aspects of my life, including my childhood and my somewhat unusual admiration for David Beckham. Ann probed me relentlessly, challenging me to explore the underlying reasons behind my thoughts and feelings. When I mentioned my admiration for Beckham, she asked why I held him in such high regard. I delved into his values, ethics, PR strategies, fashion choices, and how he managed his football career, as well as his family and patriotism. At the time, I couldn't fathom why she was digging so deeply. I suspected she might be testing my sexuality.

A few weeks later, we reconvened, and Ann unveiled my Vision Tree. It was a spider diagram with *Hand Dyed Shoe Co.* at its centre, connected by lines to numerous other circles, each representing a distinct aspect of my journey. These circles bore headings like Team, Values, Purpose, Mission, Goals, Reason, Influences, and even Dragons' Den. Lines extended from each of these circles to even more circles, adorned with concise two or three-word quotes that had emerged from my thoughts and speech. It was, without a doubt, a work of art. To this day, it proudly hangs in a frame above my desk, serving as a constant reminder of my goals.

Seeing my vision laid out on paper was akin to having a daily task list, providing me with a clear focus. During challenging times when doubts crept in, it helped me remember why I embarked on this journey in the first place and why it was crucial to persist rather than return to the safety and security of a traditional job.

The Vision Tree session also shed light on my team's roles and responsibilities. It became apparent that I was struggling with the financial aspects of my business, such as managing cash flow and VAT. These financial intricacies were not my strong suit. I possessed a basic understanding, but the moment someone delved into topics like margins or cash flow forecasts, I would break out in a nervous sweat, with hairs standing on end. I was embarrassed by my lack of comprehension. Despite the attempts of accountants, friends, business consultants, and colleagues to explain these concepts, I simply couldn't grasp them. I feigned understanding to save face. *How could I be a business owner if I couldn't grasp these fundamental aspects?* That was the nagging thought that tormented me. I confided in Ann about this, and her advice echoed what others had suggested - I needed an accountant to handle these matters for me. I agreed with her advice, despite my trepidation about the associated costs. I was still falling short of the 25-30 pairs of shoes I needed to sell to sustain my business.

The prospect of adding another expense didn't sit well with me. However, I was also deeply apprehensive about the potential consequences of mishandling finances, particularly when it came to taxes. I had heard countless horror stories about businesses being targeted by bailiffs and HMRC for unpaid taxes. I was determined not to become one of those cautionary tales. I wanted my business to operate professionally, transparently, and in accordance with the law, so I set out on a quest to find an accountant.

By the spring of 2018, my business was thriving, and I had built a loyal customer base, many of whom were fellow business owners. Among them was Gary King, a Yorkshireman and a straightforward, confident individual who had achieved success in his own career. Gary exuded an air of prosperity, and I couldn't help but be slightly sceptical of his motives when he offered to mentor me for free. However, I realised that my scepticism might have been more about my own doubts than Gary's intentions, so I agreed to join his Tendo mentorship group. I was in dire need of a mentor, someone with wisdom and experience whom I could turn to for guidance.

My first conversation with Gary revolved around my need for an accountant, as well as my desire for marketing expertise and a professionally designed website that would allow customers to customise their orders online. In my mind, this website was essential for our growth since it would enable us to sell our customisable products digitally. Gary quickly arranged meetings with a website company, an accountant, and a marketing company in which he had a stake. It seemed perfect, but the big question was how I could afford all these services.

I met with all three parties, and I was eager to collaborate with each of them. Negotiating seemed like the logical next step for a business owner. The website company, however, was well beyond my budget, quoting a price of £20,000 or more to build the software I envisioned. The marketing team, on the other hand, was more open to assisting me with one-on-one training sessions aimed at developing a marketing strategy going forward. It was an ideal arrangement. As for the accountant, I met with Diana Wylie, the owner of a firm called 'Not Just Digits.' I instantly liked Diana, and the name of her company, with its creative and quirky flair, appealed to me. Knowing that Gary worked with Diana on her own business further endeared him to me. If he could inspire such creativity in an accountancy firm, he must be exceptional.

Diana and I had a productive two-hour conversation. We quickly developed a rapport, and she was genuinely enthusiastic about my business. Her enthusiasm meant a lot to me. We delved into the details of what I needed, including year-end accounts, bookkeeping, VAT returns, and my self-assessment at year-end. There was also the matter of a small director's loan, which I didn't fully understand. Diana assured me that she would take care of all these aspects. She felt like an angel.

When she sent over the quote for her services, it amounted to around £595 per month. I was taken aback; it felt like a significant financial burden. That amount equated to selling an additional 5 pairs of shoes each month just to cover the accountant's fees. However, my strong desire to work with Diana prevailed, and Gary reassured me that with effective marketing and without the daily burden of dealing with HMRC, I would easily sell those extra 5 pairs of shoes.

By summer, my business was steadily growing. We were compelled to register for VAT because our revenue had exceeded the £80,000 threshold that mandated this step. I was pleased with this development because Diana explained that it would enable us to claim VAT back from HMRC on our purchases, which seemed like a financial win. However, what

I hadn't fully grasped was that 20% of my retail prices now went directly to the government. Unless I was purchasing more taxable products than I was selling, this meant another bill to pay on a quarterly basis. In the first month after registering for VAT, it seemed like I didn't make any profit because the VAT was due before my earnings. Gary, once again, guided me in the right direction, emphasising the need to increase my prices. I had faith in the team I had assembled – Diana and Gary were in my corner, and I had my dedicated team. If there were any issues, they would advise me. My role was simply to keep selling.

From the very beginning, LinkedIn emerged as my primary route to market. It was somewhat inexplicable; I had maintained a LinkedIn account for years without fully comprehending its potential. I had set it up back in the days when signing up for Bebo, Facebook, and MySpace was all the rage. LinkedIn was just there. It was on LinkedIn that the Northern Echo first came across my photo sitting in the river, sparking the initial idea for this incredible journey.

I had been using LinkedIn, alongside Facebook and Instagram, right from the start of my business journey. I shared photos and posts, discussing my first samples, the transformation of my daughter's old nursery into my shoe workshop, and daily videos showcasing the process of dyeing shoes and experimenting with new techniques. Over time, I had built a small but engaged following of a few thousand people. Most of my posts consistently garnered 30+ likes and numerous comments. People were incredible; they commented not only on the shoes but also on my personal qualities such as determination and authenticity. I didn't fully understand it all; I was simply being myself. I used LinkedIn almost like a blog, posting about various topics, including my frustration at seeing a grumpy server at a local store wearing her badge upside down while her employer proclaimed their attention to detail on their packaging. I was irked that the commitment to detail seemed to stop at getting dressed in the morning or during the recruitment process, so I voiced my thoughts. On another occasion, I shared a photo of a napkin that an elderly couple had handed to me as they left a coffee shop where I was conducting a meeting. The napkin contained a note wishing me success with my business but also urging me to be more considerate about the volume of my voice during public meetings. The post sparked a spirited debate. Was I wrong for being loud and inconsiderate, or were they wrong for failing to appreciate my passion and excitement? Looking back, they had a valid point, but either way, it generated compelling content.

However, a nagging issue kept me awake at night. Through my authentic and honest sharing, I had inadvertently crafted a narrative – Simon the shoemaker. I knew deep down that I wasn't truly a shoemaker; I was a shoe dyer. This distinction was why I named my business 'The Hand Dyed Shoe Co.'

Yet, many people in my following left comments describing me as a craftsman with a remarkable talent. It didn't sit right with me; it felt like I was misleading them. My social media bio even referred to me as 'Shoemaker Extraordinaire' based on a conversation I had with Ann English, who argued that no shoes could be made without Simon, effectively making me a shoemaker. This rationale calmed me for a while, and I went along with it, but in hindsight, it only perpetuated the narrative. Despite my authentic and honest approach to sharing, I felt like I was pretending to be something I wasn't.

Realising that the narrative of being a shoemaker had taken hold and was becoming a problem, I knew I had to address it delicately. If I were to simply write a post declaring, 'I DON'T MAKE SHOES, I DYE SHOES,' it might alienate a lot of people, especially those customers who had purchased shoes under the assumption that I had personally made them. This was a real dilemma for me, and by the summer, it had become even more complicated because my relationship with the Portuguese workshop was in full swing, and I wasn't personally dyeing the shoes anymore; it was being done at the workshop.

To tackle this issue head-on, I arranged a meeting with Gary King. When Gary first came to me to buy shoes for his upcoming wedding, he believed I was a shoemaker who had crafted his shoes. We met at a coffee shop in Wetherby, and I was incredibly nervous. I envisioned him becoming angry, feeling deceived. After going through some initial formalities, I decided to be forthright. I told him, 'Your shoes, mate, I didn't make them, and I didn't dye them.' I could see the disappointment on his face immediately. He didn't get angry, but he was clearly let down. We had been meeting for a few months, and I had never disclosed this before or explained my arrangement with the Portuguese workshop. I fully understood his disappointment, as I felt it too. However, I hoped he would look beyond his personal disappointment and help me rectify this narrative. After all, he was my mentor, and this conversation was not about him being a customer. After a few questions about his shoes, to his credit, he returned to the task at hand, which made me feel more at ease.

We both agreed that several steps needed to be taken to address the situation. First, we decided to create a new product line, something like 'Dyed by Simon,' which would be a more expensive premium collection of products with new packaging clearly indicating that I was responsible for the dyeing process. This would help correct the narrative that any other collection was not dyed by me. I thought it was a fantastic plan, and I immediately set to work the next day. I created new website links for the two collections and launched the brand new business model, Hand Dyed Shoe Co. version 2.

Chapter 10

Return of the Dragon

Things were going well. My little studio was active and busy. By the autumn, we were averaging 30-40 pairs per month, and I noticed that people were becoming less vocal about the whole 'Simon the shoemaker' thing. That felt better. I met Ann again for a catch-up, and inevitably, we got talking about things unrelated to work. Ann told me about her niece, Amy, and how she was having some difficulties transitioning from education. I recognised a lot of my old self in her and instantly wanted to help. I suggested that she could come down to the studio for a day or two to assist with packaging. I wanted to help because I felt like I had some wisdom and experience that could benefit her. Ann agreed it was a lovely idea, and she would love for her niece to spend some time with me.

 The day Amy arrived, she was shy. My first objective was simple: to gain her trust. To be able to help her, I needed her to open up to me, and for that, there needed to be trust. The only memory I have of our first meeting was telling her that she was welcome to leave whenever she wanted to. There were no set hours. The second thing was getting her to do things she loved, such as photography and being artistic. We organised a photo shoot with the shoes, and she really excelled. A few days turned into a week, and a week turned into two. I quickly realised that I had an employee, and although I couldn't afford one, I loved having one. She handled all the bits and pieces that I found tedious and painful, like taking items to the post office. I found jobs like that to be a massive pain in the rear. I phoned a few local colleges and inquired about apprenticeships. One of them was able to take on my new employee as a digital marketing apprentice, and as such, I could employ her for 40 hours for about £600 per month. That was music to my ears. I could have a full-time employee helping me every day, except for one college day, for just £600 per month. It was a no-brainer. We were trading fairly well, so I offered her the role, which she accepted. She became the first employee of Hand Dyed Shoe Co. Still, to this day, Amy holds that title, and while I have not seen or spoken to her for some years now, I use it as motivation for the brand. It will mean something one day if it doesn't already.

A few months after Amy officially joined the business, I moved to another, larger studio. It was a pivotal moment as we opened the doors to customers in Ushaw Historic House, a 19th-century former seminary and a truly spectacular building steeped in history. I had visions of our customers arriving at this spectacle and being utterly overwhelmed by its beauty, while slightly confused as to why there was a shoe shop (we're not a shoe shop) hidden within its rooftop. It was an unforgettable experience.

As I approached the first anniversary of my self-employment in December 2018, a lot had happened. But the overriding feeling was utter shock that I'd made it a full year without having to go to work. I was truly living the dream every single day and I was loving every minute of it. Sales were good; we were on track for £178,000 of revenue in the first 12 months. We'd settled into our new architectural surroundings and financially, it was working. I felt as though I was getting through to Amy and she was developing nicely. I started to add another chink to my vision - starting to wonder if I could create a company that was pretty much operated by a whole bunch of people who were going through tough times in their lives. We could work with the job centres and local charities to provide opportunities within the business to those who need distraction of a sense of purpose and we could become a full army of misfits. We could employ a psychologist who could be permanently available to staff or have an in-house counsellor. We could have a dedicated 'day-in-day-off' where everyone, as a team, bonds and helps each other with their issues. The thought of it made me feel great and I remember driving home faster than I should have to tell Lauren all about what I was going to do. That vision, however, soon became a dream once more when Amy suddenly left the business. I had a hunch it might come as she'd not turned in work a few days in a row and not made contact, which I felt annoyed about at the time. When she suddenly left, I figured that if my army was entirely made up of people with vulnerabilities then we would have a very difficult time retaining staff and with productivity. It needed a rethink. Right now, as we went into our second year, I just needed stability.

That requirement became even more important as January 2019 came around. I was in the studio in the midst of photographing some of our newest creations when my phone rang, displaying an unknown number. I answered, and for some reason, I instantly knew who it was: Veronica! 'I was just wondering if you had ten minutes to go over your application for Dragons' Den,' she said. You bet I did!

I wasn't nervous at all. By that time, I had attended quite a few networking events, and thanks to Colin Elrick's in-at-the-deep-end approach, I was now well-prepared when it came to talking about Hand Dyed Shoe Co. and my mission. Veronica asked me about my knowledge of the show and how much investment I'd be seeking. I couldn't recall what I had written on the application, but I confidently stated £50,000. I made that up on the spot; there was no logic behind it. When she inquired about my plans for the money, I think I mentioned that I'd invest it in the software we desperately needed to boost our online sales. She seemed impressed. In fact, the ten-minute call ended up lasting for precisely one hour and six minutes. Veronica thanked me for my time at the end of it and said she would be in touch.

As soon as I hung up, I immediately called Lauren. I couldn't contain my excitement; I told her I was going to be on Dragons' Den. I mentioned that I had just been on the phone for an hour and six minutes, and they were highly impressed with everything. I said they would be in touch with the next steps. I had barely been two minutes into my call with Lauren when Veronica's number flashed on my phone again. I abruptly cut off Lauren; I had to take this call.

'Hi Simon,' she said. 'I've just been talking to our producers, and we'd love to invite you to Manchester for an audition.'

If there's one thing I don't lack, it's confidence. If I want something, I believe I can achieve it. I am a natural problem solver, so where lots of people see barriers, I see hurdles and if I can't jump it, I will go around it. Nothing is impossible. I almost knew the day I wrote that application that I would find myself on Dragons' Den, and now I had to go to Manchester for a face-to-face audition. My body was flooded with adrenaline. Bring it on!

In a similar fashion, a few days later, I received an email

saying that I had been shortlisted for Newcomer of the Year at the North East Business Awards, alongside the Innovation Award. I had a hunch I would be shortlisted when I was filling in that application, too. It's not arrogance, but if there's one thing I've mastered over the years, it's the art of selling. Passion, love, excitement, emotion - emotion is the one thing human beings can't resist. If I can convey that emotion in an email, on an application form, or in a social media post, it will attract attention. People will feel it; they will be invested. More emails followed, including one for Newcomer of the Year at the Federation for Small Business Awards. Then a big one: I was shortlisted for the Klarna Smooothest Store Award 2019. This was special because it was a competition rather than an awards submission. Klarna, a multi-million-pound international company, was running the competition to find the UK's next big thing in retail. Out of over 500 applicants, they chose Hand Dyed Shoe Co. as one of the final eight businesses to be shortlisted.

I wouldn't go as far as to say I knew I'd win every award I was shortlisted for, but I was confident that we would win a couple, and that, for me, was incredibly exciting. I was running faster than I had ever run before at this point. There was, however, one problem in my eyes: my business was back down to one employee - just me. I needed help.

I'd often spend Sundays in the pub, being from an old northern pit village, and most weekends there were people out watching football and having a few beers. One particular Sunday, I walked into Langley Park Cricket Club and bumped into my sister, Lauren (not to be confused with my wife, Lauren). We got talking, and she began to tell me how she was a bit fed up with her current job as a carer for disabled people. It hit me like a ton of bricks. Amy had left, and I needed help, we were trading well... come and work with me.

We agreed to meet a few days later to discuss the finer details. I'm not sure what Lauren thought I was doing, but I suspect, like most people in the family, she wasn't entirely convinced it was sustainable or a proper job. It was just another one of Simon's things. She was very keen to ensure she would have a contract of employment, holiday entitlement, and all the usual employee rights. I assured her she would have all those things, of course. I like to do things properly and professionally.

She went away, and a few hours later, she called me to say she'd accept the job. I was so happy. The way I saw it, there was nothing that could go wrong as long as we stayed honest with each other. I had her back, and she had mine. I knew I was a hard worker and was committed. It was win-win, and she was never going to let me down.

At this point, I felt pretty untouchable, and it seemed like every day was an adventure. I was running faster than I had ever run before and even more convinced that the future was very bright for Hand Dyed Shoe Co. The foundations I was putting in place were very strong, and I was confident my unique business model was set to thrive, director's loan or not.

Chapter 11

Winning

By November 2018, I was flying, and so was my mother, who had been living in Tasmania, Australia, since 2002. I called her early one morning, hoping to catch her before her bedtime. When she answered, she was upset, as she often was, suffering from homesickness. She would often become quite depressed in the run-up to Christmas, especially since the grandchildren came along. But this time, I felt I could do something special. With the business thriving and a large cash injection thanks to the abundance of gift cards we'd sell in the lead-up to the festive season, I could make her Christmas memorable. I asked her if she'd like to come home for Christmas. She thought I was joking, but I wasn't. I told her I would pay for her flight and make sure she had some spending money while she was here. It was a very emotional moment for both of us. I had never spent a Christmas Day with my mam since I was about 5 years old. Here I was, over 30 years later, able to pay for her to come home and share that event with all of us as a family. I was so proud, and she was proud of me. At that moment, all my insecurities were gone. I was a hero in my mother's eyes. I was rich enough to fly her home halfway around the world and take care of her. It was the feeling I had been seeking. It was the feeling that started it all.

Christmas came and went. I only saw my mam for 2 days, Christmas Eve and Christmas Day. The rest of her time she spent with my sister Rachel in Essex, but I didn't mind. It was the most special Christmas I can ever remember, and I made it happen. I was winning.

I bought a car, a 1967 Triumph Vitesse. It was amazing, truly unique! It cost me £6,000. She was beautiful. Daisy nicknamed her Vanilla because of her creamy white paint job. The red leather interior was immaculate, and the black hood would fold down and clip behind the back seats. The walnut dashboard, chrome bumpers, and sparkling silver wheels added to her charm. She became part of our family. I'd travel to meetings and networking events in her, and she would attract attention wherever we went. We'd go on holidays, crossing the Pennines and heading over to the Lake District. Daisy would be in the back sitting alongside Fudge, our Staffordshire Bull Terrier, and Lauren in the front next to me. The Bluetooth radio would be belting out vintage songs. Vanilla was the beginning of a lifetime of memories ahead of us.

I was winning big time, and I was overflowing with happiness and pride. I visited the tattooist and had the Hand Dyed Shoe Co. logo tattooed onto my arm. Some people questioned what would happen if things went wrong or if I sold the company. But I didn't care about anything like that. I cared about this moment, this feeling, the success, and the sense of winning. I cared about the person I was becoming – a winner, a champion. The tattoo didn't symbolise shoes; it was a reminder of how this brand had given me this intense feeling of joy.

Failure couldn't have been further from my mind. I used the business to assist people I had deep compassion and admiration for. My neighbour, Chris Crook, had just left the army after over two decades of service. He wasn't in a great place mentally, suffering from PTSD, and depression, and feeling a bit lost as he adjusted to civilian life. Chris had purchased a pair of shoes from me in the early days of the business as his way of supporting my venture, and I felt compelled to do something for him. I designed a special pair of shoes for him and on the bottom of the sole, I inscribed a short poem. I don't recall the exact words, but the essence of the poem was that while the words on the sole would eventually fade as he wore them, the meaning behind them never would. The same could be said about the feelings he was experiencing; they would fade too, but the positive impact he had made on the world would always remain etched within his soul. When I gave him the shoes, it provided me with one of the greatest feelings I can recall in the history of the business, and quite honestly, probably in my life.

Then there was Tony, the local lollipop man. Tony was a wonderful person. Every morning and afternoon during Daisy's school run, he was there. He loved Hand Dyed Shoe Co., he admired my van, and he would regularly inquire about how things were going. He'd high-five Daisy at each street crossing. One day, he mentioned that he was getting married and that he wanted some of my shoes. Without wanting to prejudge, I wasn't entirely convinced he knew the price, but I didn't have the heart to question him. Sure enough, when he came for his fitting and we got to the payment part, his expression changed dramatically. He went as white as a sheet and profusely apologised for wasting my time. I reassured him, of course, that he hadn't done that at all. As he left, I immediately put his design into production. They were a stunning midnight blue pair of derby shoes, which we internally nicknamed 'Mr Angus.' I monogrammed his wedding date on the outside of the leather and delivered them by hand as a surprise when I picked up Daisy one afternoon. He was absolutely blown away. I told him they were a gift from me, a way to thank him for ensuring Daisy's safety while crossing the road every day and for making me proud of my business.

However, my favourite memory was reuniting with Mr Crabtree, my former English teacher. I felt like I could trace

Hand Dyed Shoe Co. back to his decision to place me in the top English class all those years ago. I wanted to find him and make him a pair of shoes as a token of my gratitude. It's not easy to locate a retired teacher; they're not exactly searchable on social media. By this time, he was in his late 70s, and I wasn't even sure if he was still with us. In the end, I managed to find an email address for him and reached out. I invited him to visit my studio, and when we finally met, it was a beautiful moment. I beamed as I proudly recounted my achievements. I insisted on addressing him as Mr Crabtree throughout, despite his offer to use his first name. He would always be Mr Crabtree to me. I wanted to express my gratitude. I felt I owed him a lot for what he had contributed.

Having the ability to do these things, for me, was the most remarkable aspect of having a business. It was more than just selling shoes; it was about making a positive impact, spreading kindness, and lifting people's spirits wherever I felt I could.

In the new year, I had another meeting with Diana from Not Just Digits. She informed me that my small director's loan had grown to over £20,000 over the past 12 months because our business hadn't generated enough profit to cover what I had withdrawn. It frustrated me because I found it quite perplexing. I was growing tired of hearing the term 'director's loan.' *Why couldn't they just handle it and make it right?* Diana went into great detail to explain the issues it could create in terms of the taxes I would owe and how the business wasn't generating sufficient profit for me to withdraw what I was taking. I left the meeting feeling exasperated. *Isn't this the very reason you hire accountants? To sort out these things, to help you avoid unnecessary taxes? What was wrong with the salary I was paying myself?* It wasn't an extravagant amount. I was taking £2,000 per month, and I didn't believe it was excessive. There was never a point where I didn't have £2,000 in the business account to pay myself, so I just couldn't comprehend the problem. I had to pay myself something. After all, I had worked diligently to bring the business to this point.

My pride was hurt. My ego was bruised. But, I had bigger fish to fry. I'll sort it out later.

Naturally, I used my confidence about appearing on Dragons' Den as a selling point when convincing my sister, Lauren, to join me in the business. I had booked a table for eight people at the upcoming North East Business Awards, where the company was nominated for two awards. I used that as well. I wanted Lauren to believe in the business as much as I did. Her role was primarily support-based, handling all the nitty-gritty tasks like packaging, admin, and client bookings. She was my personal assistant and the business's personal assistant rolled into one. One of her first tasks was organising the crew for the awards event. The table cost

£1,500, which was quite a sum, but we were thriving, and I believed it would be worth it. While most people invite business associates to such events to network, I took a different approach. I invited my dad, my friends Michelle and Sarah, my sisters Lauren and Pauline, their partners, and, of course, my wife Lauren. I wanted to show off a bit and have my loved ones share the moment with me; their presence meant more to me than any potential business connections.

The event was 'black tie', and since I didn't have a black suit, I opted for navy. To be honest, I wasn't entirely sure what 'black tie event' meant; I just assumed it meant dressing smartly. I felt a bit out of place in my blue attire but tried to make the best of it. I even had a suit tailored for my dad, making sure to have the leg sleeve stitched up to hold his amputated leg. I told him I would only charge him half price for the shoes. The women all looked stunning, like a table full of beautiful groupies. They were my entourage.

The guest speaker for the evening was a man named Michael Leather, and I took it as a good omen for what lay ahead. The Newcomer of the Year Award was the second prize to be announced that night, so I didn't have to wait long. As they read out the nominees, I was up against a couple of businesses I had heard of but didn't know much about. My excitement and confidence were building, and I was practically on the edge of my seat. I had already crafted my winner's speech in my head.

Then came the moment of truth... and the winner is...
THE HAND DYED SHOE COMPANY!

I can almost hear the music playing as I write this—Rag 'n' Bone Man's, 'I Am Giant.' The moment was electric. The table erupted in cheers. My dad shouted, 'Go on, son!' I stood up and walked onto the stage. The audience clapped in unison as I collected my trophy.

Overwhelmed with emotion, I felt tears welling up, but I stopped myself. I needed to be professional. I took my trophy and posed for photos with the press. As I made my way back to the table, the girls had already ordered champagne. I was elated. At that moment, it was probably the happiest I had ever been in my life. This crazy little idea I had in a sofa shop was now an award-winning business. It was my full-time job. It was providing a livelihood for my sister and bringing my mam home for Christmas. It was buying my dad a suit. That journey I made to Portugal was, at that very moment, the single best decision I had ever made in my life. I had made it.

I didn't expect to win the Innovation Award, especially when one of the other nominees had developed software that generated over a million pounds in revenue. So, I wasn't disappointed to be the runner-up in that category. For me, I had achieved what I came for—I had my trophy.

By March, I was on my way to Manchester to meet Veronica and the Dragons' Den production team. They had asked me to prepare a pitch as if I were on the show. It didn't have to be official, but I had written one and rehearsed it countless times. I travelled to Manchester with a friend. I had to be at Media City in Salford by 10:00 a.m., so the night before and that morning, I did little else but practice.

'Hello, my name is Simon Bourne, and I'm here today to request a £x,xxx investment in my bespoke shoe company...'

When I arrived, Veronica took us to her office. It wasn't quite what I had imagined. It didn't resemble what you see on TV. It was literally an office. I wasn't sure what I had expected—I knew it wouldn't be exactly like what's portrayed on TV, but I thought there might be a bit more showmanship. There was a camera, which looked like it cost no more than a few hundred quid, and that was it. After signing some forms, Veronica put me on the spot and asked me to pitch. I took a deep breath and went for it. I managed to deliver the entire pitch without stuttering. I looked the part in my quirky jacket and my glass-like shoes, and I knew it had gone well.

The whole process took about 15 minutes. Veronica emphasised that the BBC couldn't be held responsible for my mental health. I had been open about my mental health journey in my application and briefly touched on it during my pitch, explaining why creativity was so important to me.

Perhaps they were concerned that if I received heavy criticism from the Dragons, I might sue them, or maybe they were genuinely worried about my well-being. I wasn't sure. But Veronica was adamant about this point.

It wasn't something I had considered, to be honest. I know I don't handle criticism too well emotionally, but I can handle it. I think it goes back to the misconception about mental health—when people hear you suffer from anxiety or depression, they often assume you're incapable of dealing with life's challenges. I've never felt that way. I'm perfectly capable of handling criticism. I may react emotionally by getting upset (usually behind closed doors) or by standing my ground and defending myself. I might argue my point. But that doesn't mean I'm incapable of dealing with it. My reaction is my way of dealing with it. Expressing my emotions to convey how I feel about the criticism is my way of handling it. Once I've had time to process things, I can usually respond in a more balanced manner. But at the moment, I am emotional. For me, that doesn't equate to being weak or incapable. So, needless to say, I assured Veronica that I would be absolutely fine, which I would be, regardless of the outcome.

No sooner had I gotten back in the car did she call. I knew as soon as I saw the number pop up that it was her calling with the good news. I called Lauren immediately—I was barely out of Manchester. 'I am going on Dragons' Den!' I gleefully told her. And this time, there was no exaggeration.

Veronica told me they'd be in touch to go through all the due diligence, and they were looking to have me back in Manchester in the summer to film the show. I couldn't believe it, although deep down, I could. My business was going to be on TV! I was going to be on TV! Everyone and anyone who ever doubted me or thought I'd end up in jail, they were going to see me on TV, pitching to the five world-famous Dragons on prime-time BBC TV.

Things could not get any better!

Klarna called. I had been shortlisted in the final eight companies from over 500 that had been nominated. The competition, which they dubbed the 'Smooothest Stores' (sic) competition, was big budget. The eight shortlisted companies would be visited by celebrities, Millie Mackintosh and her partner, Hugo Taylor. They had made their name on a reality TV show, Made in Chelsea, and I can't profess to know much about them, but either way, I was excited that two celebrities with large social followings were going to be visiting my business. The idea was that they'd visit each business and make a showreel, which would then be shared on Klarna's social channels as well as each of the businesses' channels. Klarna would benefit from the massive exposure, and it would boost their brand awareness. Pretty clever, even if I do say so myself.

The prize for winning was £10,000 of investment, mentoring from one of Klarna's top chief executives, and, of course, the prestige of winning.

Once Hugo and Millie had visited me and the other seven businesses, the videos went out for a public vote. It was 30 days of voting, and each business campaigned to their audiences to support their ambition to win.

I knew I had a good following on LinkedIn, but many of the other companies also had strong followings on other channels such as Instagram and Facebook. I was less confident about winning this award. My main rival was a brand called Dip and Doze, a bed linen company with over 40,000 followers on Instagram. Their posts had over 50 comments and hundreds of likes. It was a big ask.

Klarna paid for myself and Lauren, along with two additional guests, to attend a huge final in Soho, London. It was a tricky decision to choose who to bring along because Lauren (my sister) was now fully embedded in the brand. Still, if there was one person I wanted to see me win an award, it was Rachel.

There has always been a special connection between Rachel and me. We were, as they say, two peas in a pod. We didn't particularly love each other growing up. She was my little sister, and she was weird. Like me, she was always in trouble, and she was a goth. She'd pierce her face in all kinds of odd places, and she'd try to snog my mates—most of whom obliged, annoyingly. She left the family home at 14 and spent some time in foster care before moving down to Scunthorpe to live with my mam. I hated that. The whole situation marked the beginning of the end for my dad and stepmam, who had very differing views on the matter. Rachel became pregnant at 15 and ended up moving to Essex with the father's mate before settling down with her new baby, my nephew, Connor, and some bloke named Phil. I was not very sympathetic; I thought she was trouble.

As we grew up, she admitted herself, she settled down. Becoming a mother at 16 was arguably the best thing that could have happened to her. It did her no harm. She ended up marrying Phil and having two more children in her twenties. She had a few jobs, but most importantly, she was a great mam to the kids. Whenever I was in trouble mentally, she was always the one person I wanted to talk to. She understood me, and as we've reached our mid-thirties, that connection is stronger than ever. We don't have to speak much, and when we do, it's pure. She's my rock, and I am hers, and no matter what life throws at us, it's quite simple, us two.

I wanted her to be there.

Lauren and I checked into a beautiful hotel, which Klarna had paid for. She looked absolutely incredible. She'd bought a sequined gold dress that sat just below her knees, paired with black pointy heels. Her hair was a golden copper, cut just past her shoulders and curled to perfection. She looked like a celebrity. When we arrived at the venue, everything was paid for. It was an open bar, and we wasted no time grabbing a couple of cocktails and mingling with the other attending businesses. There were a few celebrities in the room—singers from boy bands, DJs, models, and other influencer types. The Daily Mail had a journalist there, photographing all the guests against the Klarna backdrop. I was introduced to a CEO from Shopify, Drapers Magazine representatives, and a TV crew. The four of us sat on the end of a red curved leather sofa. The glitz and glamour were overwhelming.

As the event began to unfold, each business was showcased on the big screen. Cheers rang around the room as each new business popped up. Hand Dyed Shoe Co. was second to last, and by the time it was our turn, my heart was beating harder and faster than ever before. Hugo and Millie made a speech about how fabulous each business was before Klarna's MD took to the stage to announce the top three.

I wasn't third, and I wasn't second. That could only mean one thing—I'd won, or I hadn't come close. I was preparing my courtesy clap and non-jealous expression, hoping and praying.

'The winner is...' Hugo and Millie paused. I paused. My heart stopped. I swallowed every ounce of saliva in my mouth. And then...

'HAND DYED SHOE COMPANY!'

All moments before were eclipsed a thousand times over. Rachel jumped from her chair, launching herself at me. I didn't move; I was frozen in my seat, with both hands fixed over my open jaw. What the actual fuck? How? The room fell silent. All I could hear was Rachel's screaming. She was expressing everything I was feeling inside. Lauren mirrored me with her hands, and Phil beamed as he applauded. 'You did it, buddy!' he said.

I finally stood up and made my way to the stage to receive my trophy and the giant check. Millie gave me the microphone. I don't remember exactly what I said, but it was something along the lines of, 'I'm not an entrepreneur. I don't come from money. I am a boy from Scunthorpe, and things like this weren't supposed to happen to me.'

I went on to thank Lauren, Rachel, Phil, my team, especially my sister Lauren, and, of course, the thousands of people who had voted for me and my company. It was, literally, thousands. This was the second time in a few months I'd lived out the greatest night of my life.

Chapter 12

Dragons' Den

I had to be at the studio for 6:00 am, so I travelled to Manchester the day before. I was excited, mixed with a few nerves. I hadn't told too many people I was going to be on the show because I was under an embargo. If it got out publicly, there was a chance they might not use me in the show, and I couldn't risk that.

The night before, I practised like never before. I knew my pitch like the back of my hand. I had it down to around 45 seconds, which was pretty much perfect in terms of what the producers wanted. I still didn't know how much I was going to ask them for or how much equity I was prepared to give away. I didn't really know what I wanted the money for. What I wanted, more than anything, was the experience. I wanted to be on Dragons' Den, come what may.

When I arrived, my first job was to set up my stall in the foyer of the set. They wanted it to look exactly how I wanted it to look once the cameras were rolling. There were eight businesses there in total, all doing the same thing. Once I had set up my stand, the producers came around to each one and made tweaks. Things that were too shiny or might interfere with the cameras had to be removed. They refined it but didn't change a lot. I was happy. They asked me then what my intentions were in terms of my ask. I told them £20,000 for 10%. There was no science behind it. There was no valuation that I'd put on my business. I just made it up. For me, the business wasn't worth a great deal right now, and I hoped that what they were going to invest in was the potential of it - and, if I'm honest, me. The producers weren't keen, though, and they asked to change it to £70,000 in return for 15%. I don't know why they wanted me to do that, but I went with it anyway. As I said, I wasn't too fussed about the deal; I was more interested in getting an offer, irrespective of what it was. I suspect that across the eight businesses, they were trying to offer some variation, and perhaps a few of us were all pitching for the same amount of money.

I left my stand and was taken to a holding room. From there, we weren't allowed out unless we were accompanied by a member of the security team. Each business would be called one by one to do their pitch. They then told us that each business would probably take around 2-3 hours before the next one was called as they changed around the set and, I assume, touched up Tukur Suliman's makeup. It didn't take a genius to work out that it meant that some of us were in for a very long day.

It seemed to take forever. I ended up being business number seven. By this time, I was red hot with my pitch, having spent barely a minute throughout the day doing anything other than practising to the green room wall. I didn't feel tired, despite the early start. Adrenaline was pumping around my body, keeping me highly charged.

I was called at around 4:30 pm. It was my turn. I had no idea what had happened to the six businesses before me. You don't see them again once they've done their thing. So, everything I was about to experience was brand new.

It might sound stupid, but I had imagined that the whole thing was filmed in an old, dingy warehouse. It's not. It's just a set. But what I would say is that it's a brilliantly done one. I'd never been on a TV set before, but the level of detail, from the fans to the artificial windows with artificial daylight projecting through them, is so cool. I was invited to walk onto the set and around the corner, which most viewers would be familiar with. It's the part where you see the pictures on the wall of the Dragons, and their nerve-ridden victim has the opportunity to pour themselves a glass of water before entering the lair. A traffic light is visible above the camera, and I was instructed to wait on the taped cross for the green light. I stood there for what felt like 30 minutes. It may well have been, I'm not sure. The green light came on, and I then walked around the corner to the lift, where I pressed the button. Again, I waited. Once in the lift, you wait some more, around ten more minutes. Eventually, the doors opened on the other side of the lift, and there they were. Five Dragons, sitting in their chairs next to the huge wads of cash just piled up, pens in hand, awaiting their meal.

It's much smaller than it looks on TV. The camera operators are spread around the floor, but you can't see them much because of the dimly lit den. Or at least, I didn't notice them. I only had eyes for the Dragons. As I made my way across the dance floor, I heard Tukur Suliman utter the word shoemaker. I knew my first challenge before I'd even opened my mouth. This was going to be another Gary King moment.

I found my mark on the floor, looked up, took a big gulp, and went into the pitch. 'Hello, Dragons. My name is Simon Bourne...' I got to my second paragraph and stuttered. I'd practised a million times, but my mind went blank for a brief moment. The nerves got me. You literally get one go at this - there is no opportunity to retake a scene or have another go. It knocked me sideways a little, but I got back on track thanks to a supportive smile from Sara Davies. I really wanted to get my purpose across in the pitch, so I spoke about my insecurities and anxieties. I spoke about how creating a product for myself, a one-off thing, helped me feel individual and comfortable in my own skin. I went on to talk about how with their support, I wanted to open hidden boutique studios in old barns, churches, and unique locations across the UK and beyond. I thought they'd love that.

I knew my numbers and I was confident. I'd romanticised a lot in the build-up about which Dragons I would choose; thinking that I would have a choice of a few. I had considered how I would negotiate, and if I'd negotiate. I wanted Peter Jones. He always came across as a lovely man and someone I'd like to work with. I felt like we'd work well together, and his man-management skills would be well suited for me. As I finished my pitch, I told the Dragons that I'd made them each a pair of shoes that I felt expressed their style and individuality. Peter's were a stunning pair of deep tobacco-coloured double monk straps. I'd given them an extra polish before I went in. They reacted well. Peter put his straight on and jumped out of his chair to stand next to me. He was huge! I'm 6' 1" tall, but Peter felt like a giant next to me. It's commonly known that he's a tall man, but until he's standing next to you in his den, you don't realise quite how tall he is. He was complimentary; he said they fit well and he loved them. Tej Levani jumped out of his seat. I'd created him a lovely pair of Derby brogues, a combination of tan with a blue suede bridge. They looked great. He moonwalked across the den floor, commenting about the slipperiness. They were slippy on the wooden floor, as fresh leather soles usually are. Overall, I couldn't have wished for a better start, despite the stutter. Sara Davies opened, 'Excellent pitch,' she said with a beaming northern gaze of familiarity. She'd picked up on my accent. We bonded, I felt, almost immediately. She'll offer, I was thinking to myself.

The questioning was pretty clean early on. There was nothing too taxing or anything I felt I'd tripped up with. It helped as I relaxed into the process. The Dragons were keen to understand the bespokeability of the shoes and how our retail experience worked. With each answer I got, I felt stronger and more confident in what was unfolding. Deborah Meaden has made millions from the holiday industry. She'd been on the show since its inception and she'd developed a reputation for being direct. She was sitting dead centre, and as she asked me questions, it felt sharp. I didn't get a good vibe from her. She asked me if she could look at my brochure, so I took it from my display, walked to her seat, and handed it to her before moving back to my marker. Tukur jumped in with a question while Deborah flicked through.

We were about half an hour in when suddenly, the mood changed. Tukur asked how many pairs of shoes I made a month and how the business could potentially scale if I was making all the shoes. I was defiant in my answer. I was excited to counter. I told him I didn't actually make the shoes and that we had a supply chain already set up in Portugal that could take volume into the thousands. I answered with authority and pride, assuming he'd love it. But, he didn't.

'Oh!' he emphatically scoffed, 'You don't make the shoes?' I immediately went into defence. 'No, I have designed the shoes, created the business model, built the supply chain and the sales model. I've put the foundations in to allow it to grow beyond the bedroom business that it started as.'

He didn't look impressed. 'You're a marketing gimmick,' he returned. My heart sank. He went quiet. Deborah returned, supporting Tukur's disappointment that I wasn't the shoemaker they thought I was. 'That's why you didn't want to give me your brochure,' she said. I didn't like that at all. I squirmed. It pissed me off actually. I didn't not want to give her my brochure at all. She asked, then I picked it up and I walked over to give it to her. I didn't hesitate or even comment when she asked. I felt like she said it for the cameras. It made a bit more drama for the show. At that point, my bruised ego dismissed working with her, even if she did offer.

From here, we got into the numbers. It was the numbers that I thought would trip me up. I was pretty good on them - I knew my margins and I knew my profit and loss. I could talk about operational costs and all that jargon. I was nervous about the Director's Loan. I didn't want them to know about that because I still didn't understand it. But numbers, I'd seen it a thousand times on the show; it's where the Dragons really get their claws out. Tukur quizzed. I could tell he was looking for his way out. He wanted me to be 'the shoemaker,' and because I wasn't, he just started jabbing. As I answered each of his questions, he returned with another one, scribbling on his pad before chucking his pen in between the pages and putting it back on his side table.

Peter asked a few more questions about the supply chain, assessing capability and resources. He asked me if I had any shares in the workshop. I didn't, but I told him that I'd love to buy it one day. He then asked me how my shoes compared to those of Herring Shoes. For some reason, my mind went blank and I couldn't think of who Herring Shoes was. I knew all the big ones: Loakes, Church's, Cheaney, Crockett & Jones, Barkers. Herring Shoes; I just couldn't fathom the name. I considered bluffing, but I was petrified that they'd see through that, so I just replied with 'I don't know them, sorry.' He wasn't impressed. He picked up the shoes he'd taken off and turned them over to reveal the Herring Shoes brand on the bottom. *Fuck,* I thought.

I launched into a second pitch, talking about my vision for a franchised business model and a country loaded with Shoe Guys who would all be trained to guide customers through this exciting retail proposition. Again, they cut me off. 'Didn't you say 70% of your orders were online,' said Peter Jones. I had said that in my opening gambit. I was trying to impress them that we could scale the business online as much as anything. I believed that all retail entrepreneurs would only really be interested if there was an online model which could be multiplied quickly with some search engine optimisation or pay-per-click spend. I'd tripped myself up.

I desperately changed the topic towards how we'd build a company that was supportive of mentally vulnerable people, creating an environment where our employees could thrive where perhaps in other companies, they couldn't. I was hoping the niceness of my intent would cut me some slack. Wide-eyed, I defended the supply chain, telling them that if it was just me and I was doing everything, then there would be no business. It would be nothing more than a hobby. What I'd built was a brand and a business model that was scalable and that they should join me on the journey. Deborah cut me off. 'Let me make this simple,' she said. 'I don't think this is an authentic business and it's not something I could invest in, so I'm out.' It was, as the show's narrator Evan Davies would describe in the final edit, the first blow. Tukur jumped straight in to follow her exit. I didn't fight or argue with either of them. I just smiled, nodded, and focused on maintaining a humble, dignified response.

Peter came next. He and Tej hadn't asked a great deal. The Herring Shoes cock up bothered him. That one stung. As Tej began speaking, I was braced for the next token nod. But, his tone was different. 'I don't mind the Portugal thing,' he said. He commented that they make great shoes out there, which they do. He told me I'd done well to get it to this point and that he understood why I'd done things the way I had. I exhaled a huge breath of relief. I sniffed an opportunity as he started to dig up the old ground around the bespokeability. He quizzed me deeply about the level of options and fitting. He dug into the online statistics and how we replicate our in-store business model digitally. He was eagerly noting down my answers in his book when Sara Davies took over. She looked up, and smiled at me, and I knew what was coming. She said she wanted nothing more than to invest in a good North East-based crafty business, but unfortunately, that's not what this was, so disappointingly, she was out. I gave her my smile, gave her my appreciative nod, and made a little heart sign with my hands. No hard feelings, I was trying to say.

There was one Dragon left. Tej. He was, in truth, the last one I'd have chosen if I was given my pick. He's a lovely man, but I always thought he was a little bit nerdy. He's big in the probiotics industry, and that's something I've never understood much about or had much interest in. It's all a bit intense for me. I was staring at him with smitten eyes and gritted teeth in anticipation of where his mind was. He asked me a few more questions, looked down at his book, and then looked back up at me. 'I haven't got any issues with what you've done,' he said. 'I would have done the same thing.' I inhaled. He paused. 'Unfortunately, I don't think there's enough there, so for that reason, I'm out.'

No offers. I was sure I'd get one, at least. I thought I'd get a few. Perhaps my confidence had turned to arrogance. Maybe the awards and the wins had gone to my head. I thanked them, turned 180 degrees, and made my way back to the lift. I instantly thought about calling Lauren to tell her I had failed. She never said it, but I knew she believed I'd get an offer too, as did my mom. As I walked out, my first instinct was to provide my response to a camera waiting for me on the other side of the lift. I held back the tears. I admitted I was disappointed but delivered a speech of defiance. I would be back, and I would continue pursuing my ambition. As soon as the camera turned away, I began to cry. I wasn't bawling my eyes out; I was simply overwhelmed with emotions. Some of the crew asked me how I felt off-camera, and I confided that I was most disappointed about the authenticity comment. Over the past few years, I had bared my soul, and spoken publicly about anxiety and mental health, all in an effort to make a difference. I had invested a lot of time into Amy and my mission to improve lives. Therefore, to have my authenticity questioned was painful.

It was around 8:00 pm by this point. I had spent approximately 90 minutes in the den, presenting and fielding questions. It was going to be a long drive back to Durham. I called Lauren as soon as I left the car park. Initially, I was eager to tell her that I had received an offer and that Peter Jones was now my business partner. However, when I informed her that I hadn't received an offer, she reacted as any supportive spouse would. She commended me for making it onto the show and achieving something none of our acquaintances had ever done. She reminded me that regardless of the outcome, my business would be exposed to millions of people, which was a fantastic opportunity. She seemed to echo the modesty I had feigned before I left, where I pretended not to mind much whether I secured an investment or not. But, truthfully, I did mind, and her compliments didn't provide much solace. In my mind, I had failed.

 I had assured Veronica that I would be fine, and I was. I wasn't on the brink of disaster or some form of mental breakdown. I was merely upset and disappointed in myself. I was also very anxious, mainly about which parts of that 90-minute recording would make it into the final edit. Nonetheless, I was okay. I just wanted to get back home, back to Lauren and Daisy.

Chapter 13

Growth

It took a few weeks to get over the experience. I had been mentally preparing for it for months during the due diligence process. I had fantasised about the future and how Peter Jones would hold my hand as we grew Hand Dyed Shoe Co. into a globally successful company. I had even dreamed about owning a Porsche. The post-Dragons' Den feeling was somewhat similar to the one I experienced after my wedding – a period of low mood and emptiness. You build up this monumental event in your head as the most significant thing that will happen in your life, and then it's over in a flash. Then what? It left me feeling down for a while.

The summer of 2019 came, and we went on a two-week holiday, travelling to Barcelona and then catching a train to Toulouse, where we stayed at the foot of the Pyrenees for seven days. It was just what I needed to recharge my batteries. During this time, I read the book 'Shoe Dog' by Phil Knight, the founder of Nike. I'm not much of a reader due to my short attention span, but the combination of sunshine, downtime, and the subject matter piqued my interest.

I must have driven Lauren insane as I recounted almost every chapter because it felt like I was reading my own autobiography. Knight talked about how he grew Nike into a global brand by building successful supply chains out of Japan and later Taiwan. He openly discussed his insecurities and how he built a team around him to compensate for his skill gaps. For me, it was like reading a step-by-step guide on what I needed to do with Hand Dyed Shoe Co. It wasn't technology I needed; it was people.

When I returned, I decided to invest the £10,000 I received from Klarna in a marketing agency. They connected me with a London-based firm that specialised in social media marketing. If Klarna, a company that spends millions on marketing, recommended them, they had to be good.

The run-up to Christmas that year was chaotic, both in the business world and at home. Lauren was pregnant with our second baby, right in the midst of her Midwifery degree. There was pressure on me to earn a bit more money to make ends meet. The business was doing well, and there was always money in the bank at the end of each month. Penny arrived ten days early on the 15th December 2019, though her due date was Christmas Day. I was scared to become a dad again. I never gave myself much credit when it came to parenthood and often compared myself to my friends and other dads on social media. I didn't excel in the routine stuff like bedtimes or diaper changes. Instead, I preferred to take them out in the car. I viewed that preference as a shortcoming. I felt like I couldn't handle being a dad; I lacked patience and was terrible at all the typical dad tasks. My desire to take them on car trips felt like an excuse to escape from the fundamental aspects of fatherhood.

We had waited seven years to have another baby due to my anxiety. The idea of adding more responsibilities to my already unenthusiastic list of parental duties made me feel worse about myself. I used the business as a reason to avoid the responsibilities of being a dad. I had an empire to build, and I needed to be fully committed. I bought into the belief that success required extreme dedication, working late, meditation, reading books, listening to podcasts from famous speakers, having a world-class mentor, and an executive business coach. I believed I needed an investment. These were the thoughts that consumed me during this time. I was obsessed with the business; it had to work, it had to grow.

I visited Portugal in early December. I wanted to take the team at the factory out and pay for dinner as a thank you for what had unquestionably been the greatest year of my life. Midway through our meal, I tapped my glass, stood up, and emotionally delivered my speech. I couldn't have achieved the North East Business Award or made it on Dragons' Den without the support of this amazing team. I expressed how incredibly happy I was. Well, I was until the €1,000 bill arrived at our table.

By the time Penny arrived, I was pretty exhausted. We were on track for over £250,000 in sales for 2019. It had been a whirlwind twelve months. With the help of the agency, we sold 170 gift vouchers in the run-up to Christmas, and we had nearly £30,000 in cash in the bank. It wasn't profit since we would have costs when those vouchers were redeemed throughout 2020, but having that much money in the bank felt amazing. In addition to this, we had just sold our house and were preparing to move as a family of four. Life was good.

As the new year approached, with momentum on our side, I decided it was time to grow. I explored various ways to raise the necessary funds. My preference was to secure an investor because what I needed more than anything was guidance. I wanted someone to guide me through the process. However, I didn't know where to start. I wasn't sure how much I needed or what amount of equity was reasonable. I feared being taken advantage of, and I didn't have an immediate contact I could turn to for advice. In addition to this, I was regularly contacted by brokers and lenders offering to invest in my business, but I didn't want to go down that uncertain path. Instead, I chose to apply for a loan through Funding Circle, a company I had seen on television and considered more trustworthy.

I initially applied for £50,000, but when I was approved, the representative on the phone informed me I was eligible for up to £100,000. The idea of having £100k at my disposal was tempting, but I settled on borrowing £70,000. My plan was to use this money to hire a marketing executive internally. I believed that having an in-house marketing expert would significantly boost our social reach, brand awareness, and ultimately, our sales. Sunderland University was offering a deal where they would cover a percentage of the first year's salary if we recruited a graduate, which provided us with a bit of extra budget. At the beginning of the year, we began advertising the position. This felt like a significant step toward achieving my goal, and I couldn't help but think about the Porsche.

We received around 30 applications, and after reviewing them, we narrowed down the list to approximately 5 candidates whom we invited for interviews. We asked them to create a hypothetical campaign for us based on our brand tone, believing it would quickly reveal which newly graduated candidate understood our concept best.

On the day of the interviews, Lauren (my wife) and I prepared ourselves. One candidate stood out immediately: Laura Raister. Her application was exceptionally well-written, and she had even built her own website showcasing her photography and case studies. Her social media profiles demonstrated creativity, and she had a genuine passion for data.

She ticked many boxes, and both Lauren and I were excited to see how she performed in the interview. She happened to be the last candidate scheduled to interview at 1:30 pm. Surprisingly, she was the only one who showed up.

Laura made a fantastic first impression. Her friendly demeanour put me at ease, which was rather ironic. She performed exceptionally well during the interview, so well that we forgot to ask her to deliver her brand presentation. Lauren and I didn't need to exchange many words to recognise the gut feeling we both had. I waited a few hours before giving Laura a call that evening to offer her the job, with a start date of 24th February 2020.

This was a game-changer.

Before Laura's first day, I decided to invest in a new camera gadget designed to facilitate the creation of quick, authentic content for platforms like Instagram. Reels were just starting to gain traction, and I believed that video would become increasingly important in the years to come. After she had signed her contract, I sent this gadget to her in the post along with a 'good luck in your new job' card. My goal was to make her feel welcome, especially since she was joining a brother-sister team.

Additionally, I arranged what I believed would be a coffee-making experience day that the three of us could attend during her first week. However, it turned out to be more of a coffee-tasting day, which, while interesting, wasn't quite the experience I had in mind, especially considering that Laura didn't drink hot beverages.

Our trade was flourishing, we had a new team in place for 2020, and I was laying the groundwork for what would eventually become the Hand Dyed Shoe Co. culture. At that moment, it felt like there was very little that could hinder our progress, not even the nasty cold that was spreading across Europe in those early months of 2020.

Chapter 14

Pandemic

The first time I took the COVID-19 pandemic seriously was when we learned that Italy had gone into lockdown. Until then, it had been one of those distant events you see on the news, like famine, war, or natural disasters. While tragic, these events always felt worlds away from our daily life here in the UK. It's not arrogance, but perhaps ignorance.

When Italy entered lockdown, it made me contemplate the possibility that we might also have to face a lockdown. However, when I say contemplate, it was more of a passing thought than a serious consideration. I didn't believe it would actually happen. I remember watching Italians on their balconies playing musical instruments and forming impromptu bands on the edges of their apartments, playing to the empty streets below. I also saw a video of Milan's deserted Square, a place I had visited with Lauren in 2008. It was surreal, like something out of a zombie film. Even then, I still thought that if the Coronavirus reached our shores, we would somehow overcome it. There was no way our country would stop working and simply stay at home.

One of Laura's initial tasks, almost on the day she started, was to prepare for my upcoming appearance on Dragons' Den, scheduled to air on Sunday, 3rd March 2020. We had only ten days to get ready. By that time, we had begun collaborating with a workshop in the UK, and I wanted to use the Dragons' Den platform to announce our new Made in Britain collection to address criticisms about my more continental supply chain. We worked tirelessly to create the necessary content. I was also recording numerous interviews with local radio and TV crews in anticipation of the show, wanting to make the most of this opportunity.

I was more nervous on that Sunday than I had ever been before. I knew that the Dragons' Den episode had recorded 90 minutes of material, giving them plenty of content to shape the narrative as they pleased. My biggest fears were centred around the potential embarrassment of not recognising Herring Shoes and the exposure of all my margins and numbers to the world, including my customers. It didn't sit comfortably with me, but I was also excited. This was my big television debut, after all.

A few friends gathered at my house, and we ordered pizzas for the premiere, but I couldn't eat due to nerves. As the show began, I felt acutely aware that the world was watching—my parents, siblings, friends, people from school, customers, old teachers—all recognising the name, Simon Bourne. I was the second act on the show, and given the law of averages, most viewers probably guessed that things wouldn't go smoothly for me. The segment lasted eight minutes, condensing almost 2 and a half hours of filming.

Surprisingly, they didn't include the part about Herring Shoes, nor did they reveal my numbers. The opening minutes portrayed a sense that I couldn't fail, with the Dragons expressing interest in my shoes and brand. However, around halfway through, the tone shifted, particularly when the Portugal issue came to light. I had expected that part to be used, as it was the reason I lost three of the Dragons. Overall, I wasn't overly disappointed with the edit, and I felt they had been kind in terms of how bad they could have made me look. My phone exploded with messages from old customers, friends, and family offering their thoughts and feedback, which was mostly positive. I felt immensely proud—I had been on Dragons' Den. While I hadn't secured their backing, I had successfully appeared on the show.

Moreover, our website experienced a surge in traffic, to the point where it crashed briefly due to the high number of hits. We booked around 30 appointments and sold several pairs of shoes online that night. We also announced the Made in Britain collection and sent out a press release about the news. I didn't get much sleep that night.

The following week, it became increasingly apparent that the Coronavirus situation was getting more serious. People were dying in the UK, and rumours circulated about the possibility of a lockdown. It all seemed surreal, and I struggled to comprehend the unfolding events. Despite my own doubts and fears, I reassured Lauren and Laura, who were anxious, particularly Laura, who had recently joined the company. I recalled a quote from Walt Disney about not participating in a recession, and I decided to adopt a similar attitude. I assured the team that we would not be taking part in the Coronavirus crisis and aimed to provide strong, confident, and reassuring leadership during this challenging time.

By 23rd March 2020, the country went into lockdown. We were instructed by the Prime Minister that we could not leave our homes for anything more than an hour per day and only for essentials such as food. The other 23 hours of your day must be spent in our homes. It was utterly crazy. I figured at this point we'd have to do this perhaps for the following 2 weeks. I told my team to work from home; that they'd get paid in full and they need not worry. By the time the furlough scheme was announced, where the Government would help to cover the salaries of those who couldn't work, I'd realised that Laura wasn't eligible because she started with us after the last pay run. I was frustrated, but I didn't want to lose her. She was, as far as I was concerned, a fantastic asset for the company and I'd just found her. I had just started this new journey of growth and she was very much part of it.

Almost overnight, we'd gone from revenues of £50,000 per month, to barely £3,000. Nobody was spending and the money we could generate was largely based on goodwill. Without the ability to meet our customers, we simply couldn't sell. I was more concerned, but I still wasn't worried. The loan was in the bank and I knew we had that to fall back on. It wasn't ideal, but it would buy us time.

As the weeks became months, we'd reverted to video call meetings and doing what we could to try to keep the wheels turning. We tried some promotional giveaways and we made some appeals to our existing customers to come back again. Some did, but it was sporadic. I was paying both Lauren and Laura their full wages, as well as paying my mother-in-law. I still didn't feel overly panicked and for large parts of the first lockdown, I enjoyed myself. It felt like an extended period of paternity leave, with Penny only a few months old by the time it started and I was enjoying spending time with her. I knew we were dipping into the loan to be able to keep things going but I felt like it was under control. We were set to have a few months of bad trade, but the loan gave us the safety net to keep everyone in jobs and with no need to overly panic. We weren't taking part, after all.

By the time the end of June arrived, there was a change in my mindset. I began struggling at home with the monotony of a one-hour daily walk, the torture of daytime television and the lack of sport to distract my mind from the business.

I woke up one morning and I didn't get out of bed. I just lay there. Lauren assumed I was just having a lie-in, but I wasn't. I was crying. I was thinking about suicide. The fear was starting to kick in. I knew we'd spent around £10,000 of the loan and with no sign of the pandemic's end, reality was starting to set in. This has to change soon, I thought. The fact I couldn't fathom how to innovate fast enough to get our revenues back up was frustrating me and I felt trapped. I found myself becoming increasingly stressed and agitating to be around. The novelty was very much wearing off and I just wanted to get back to work. The team was working from home, but it was difficult for them to make headway with much. They were in the same boat as me. We just had to try to be patient. I didn't let on to the team that I was starting to struggle. I didn't want them to think I was worried but the thing with momentum is that it is equally as powerful for you as it is against you, if your mindset isn't right. The lockdown had killed our upward momentum almost overnight and with our hands now tied, I could feel how momentum was now slowing.

As August arrived, we were permitted to return to work, albeit with mandatory mask-wearing. While customers could visit, it was far from the bustling activity we were accustomed to. Appointments were often cancelled at the last minute due to the track and trace system, which required individuals to stay home if they had come into contact with someone who tested positive for COVID-19. Additionally, as part of the Government's Eat Out to Help Out scheme, team members frequently had to stay home as the scheme encouraged people to engage in gatherings, which posed a challenge for us. We just couldn't get going.

The situation worsened rapidly as our loan continued to dwindle. We were using the loan to cover expenses like rent, wages, VAT, PAYE, and suppliers. Behind the scenes, I was growing increasingly anxious but shielded my staff from the full extent of the problem. It was crucial that they remained unaware, especially considering that Lauren was my sister. I felt lost, and uncertain about what the future held and how to address the situation. Each day felt like a repetition of the previous one.

Christmas in 2020 was a subdued affair compared to previous years. Restrictions limited the number of people allowed at the festive dinner table. We had just emerged from the second lockdown, which had been implemented with a more localised approach. Unfortunately, this didn't work in our favour, as customers from outside County Durham were unable to visit us due to our local lockdown status. Much of our trade typically came from visitors travelling to our location. The third lockdown, in early 2021, marked over a year of ongoing challenges. During that time, we managed to sell approximately £50,000 worth of shoes, which represented a staggering 74% drop in sales. Our operational costs had risen over 70% since 2019, largely due to increased salaries and various marketing commitments I had taken on in an attempt to revitalise the business. At this point, the loan was nearly exhausted, and I had only around £10,000 in cash reserves, which was less than our monthly overhead.

In April 2021, we were finally permitted to return to work, and I was ecstatic about it. I anticipated that things would gradually return to some semblance of normalcy. However, that wasn't the case. While we did start to see customers again, it was only a fraction of the numbers we used to serve before the pandemic. A typical Saturday in 2019 would involve back-to-back appointments, often totalling six or seven. Despite my efforts to open up the diary on weekends, we weren't receiving as much interest. There were only sporadic appointments here and there.

As we began to work through our situation and assess our options, Laura informed me that she had received another job offer, which she intended to accept. While I couldn't help but feel disappointed, given the significant support I had provided her during the pandemic, I understood her decision. If I were in her position, I would have made the same choice. The larger problem I now faced was that I had spent £70,000 to keep the business afloat, and with Laura now leaving, we had little to show for it. We found ourselves in an exceedingly vulnerable and challenging market. There were few options available to me other than to persevere, continue trading, and wait for a return to some semblance of pre-2020 conditions. And then, almost out of nowhere, it happened—a lifeline emerged.

Amongst the long and tormenting days, there was still reason for optimism. I'd been introduced to Charles Clinkard in April 2021 - just after the end of the last lockdown. He was the leader of the shoe retail giant that bore the same name. Clinkard himself was a third-generation leader of the brand that was formed in the 1920s. It's a huge British brand which at the time, adorned over 30 high streets around the UK, not to mention their incredible online presence. I'd looked into their accounts and they'd reported anywhere between £25m - £40m worth of sales across the last decade; and that's in a very tricky market. They sold Loakes, Trickers, Barkers and Crockett & Jones. All the big shoe brands. I'd given Charles a tour of my studio in the middle of the two lockdowns. He seemed to really like what he saw and a few days later, he introduced me to Tim Payne, the company's Managing Director. I invited Tim to visit, which he duly did, and I guided him through the Hand Dyed Shoe Co. experience. He too seemed very impressed with the brand and how we did things. Conversations soon turned to how we could collaborate. *This was it,* I thought. This was the turning point I was waiting for. Almost instantly, I could picture it. My brand on a shelf alongside historic and timeless brands like Loake. My brand in every major city around the UK. Sales are coming in every day. Hundreds of them. I was picturing the awards. I was dreaming about the brand being spoken about as people eulogise about Loake or Church's. I was fantasising about how Loake or Oliver Sweeney would come along and one day, they'd want to buy the company from me for a seven-figure-sum. I'd be a self-made millionaire! Not bad for a kid who was destined for jail as a teenager, I obnoxiously thought to myself. If I could prove it works in Leeds, then Clinkards would put Hand Dyed Shoe Co. in all of their stores around the UK and we would be selling hundreds of pairs per week all around the country. We would soon be able to pay back that loan. And, well, if it didn't, I would kill myself. That was the trade-off that was going on in my mind. Those were the stakes.

Tim and I agreed that we would each invest £10,000 in the renovation of an old storeroom in the rooftop of the Leeds shop. Clinkards would support the project with a substantial promotion on their social media channels, which collectively had around 20,000 followers, and through their email database. The £10,000 investment was a significant step up from the DIY renovation of my existing studio, where I painted and furnished the space with items sourced from car boot sales and charity shops. However, this professional upgrade was necessary for Clinkards to view me as an equal in the business world. So, despite knowing that it represented nearly all the funds I had in the bank at that moment, I agreed to the investment.

In the following months, trade continued to disappoint, and we were consistently losing money month after month. I resorted to using my business credit cards to extend our cash flow by another 30 days. My focus was entirely on the Leeds store. I firmly believed that once we opened the store, everything would turn around. Sales would start pouring in, and we would gradually recover. By the end of September, the shop fitters had arrived, constructing stud walls and decorating according to my specifications. They did an exceptional job, and we officially opened the Leeds store on 27th September 2021. Both Laurens came down to help set everything up and put the final touches on the room. The store looked spectacular. Although I was envious, wishing it were my studio, I trained Marcus Wright, the store's manager, on how everything worked, guiding him through the appointment process and showing him the technology.

When I got home, I was utterly exhausted. It was a strange feeling. I had been so excited about this new collaboration and the potential rewards it offered. However, I found myself sitting with a negative balance in my business bank account, a £70,000 loan that was gone, and over £17,000 in credit card debt. There was also barely any incoming trade to speak of. I couldn't help but remember the night I won the Klarna award and how invincible I had felt. It was like riding a wave of arrogance. Opening the Leeds store was undoubtedly a significant moment, but I didn't feel like celebrating. Nevertheless, I knew we should. I hoped that it would indeed be a turning point, and it deserved recognition.

I walked to our local store and bought a bottle of champagne. When I tried to pay, my card was declined. Luckily, I had £30 cash in my pocket, which was just enough to buy it. Lauren and I sat at our dining room table and drank it. I photographed the bottle and posted it on social media. I wanted the world to know how excited I was about this new opportunity and achievement. But, at the same time, I felt sick that I was lying to people, giving them the perception of success when, in fact, I was, at that moment, a debt-ridden gambler. The taste of the champagne wasn't particularly enjoyable.

Chapter 15

Loser

The invoice from the shop fitters arrived, totalling £20,000. Clinkards paid their agreed half and forwarded it to me for my share. I didn't have the money. I chose to ignore it, pretending I hadn't seen it. I was hoping that buying time would produce something.

During the first week in Leeds, I commuted to the store every day. I managed to conduct 11 appointments that first week, generating around £8,000 in revenue, which was a promising start. Most of these customers were drawn in through our internal marketing efforts, particularly my LinkedIn profile and the excitement I had generated. Marcus observed each appointment, and at the end of that week, I handed over the reins.

Clinkards' marketing initiatives had not fully taken off yet, but they were preparing their social media push, and email marketing, and had agreed to feature the brand in their shop window. I was thrilled about that prospect – my shoes and brand displayed in the window of a bustling city high street. It couldn't happen soon enough for me, as I needed a boost sooner rather than later. However, it seemed to take forever. It wasn't until the end of October, another month later, that things started to click and they began actively marketing the brand. Unfortunately, it was another month closer to a follow-up call from the shop fitters regarding their outstanding £10,000.

My vision for how it would work was that Marcus and his team would regularly promote this exciting new collaboration to the gentlemen shopping for Loakes or Barkers in the store. Marcus would escort customers up the vintage lift to the second floor, where upon opening the doors, they would be enveloped by the alluring scent of hand-dyed leathers. They would be unable to resist the unique experience and the desire to create a one-of-a-kind item. After all, these customers loved their shoes; that's why they had come into a shoe shop. Unfortunately, reality didn't align with my vision. In that first month, Marcus only conducted two appointments, both of which I had generated through LinkedIn. It simply wasn't enough to cover the shop fitters' bill.

Clinkards' marketing team finally installed the window display in early November, but little changed. There was no sudden influx of orders. Marcus remained optimistic during our conversations, assuring me that customers in the store showed interest in the shoes and the concept when pitched to them. However, he had yet to take a single customer up the lift, let alone make a sale. I visited the store a few times to observe and try to understand what was happening. I even spoke to customers on the shop floor, introducing them to the concept above their heads. The feedback I received was that while the idea was intriguing, going up an unfamiliar lift to an unknown location seemed odd rather than unique. I realised there was a fine line, and my previous celebration with champagne had come across as arrogant.

It was by the end of November that I realised our approach, with a quirky speakeasy hidden away in the rooftops, was probably a mistake. A costly mistake. A £10,000 mistake.

Not for the first time, I woke up feeling sick with worry. I found myself regularly staring outside, and no matter what was happening, it felt dark. I remember looking at the trees dancing on the green outside our bedroom window. The leaves were crisp red, and the ground was littered with golden yellows and orange tones. Within seconds of that moment of awareness, I'd turn away and slam the curtains closed. These trees weren't mine; they were at risk. They served as a reminder of my greed. *Who did I think I was, believing I could be more than a working-class kid from Scunthorpe?*

The shop fitters called me, and the lady on the other end of the line said, 'We're just chasing up payment of your half of the invoice.' I tried to bluff my way through it, apologising for the delay and assuring them I'd get it sorted the next week. In reality, I didn't have the money, and there was no clear source of income in the next seven days. Panic set in; I was terrified that Charles and Tim would find out about this and pull the plug on our collaboration. It was far from the start I had been hoping for, or rather, praying for.

During November, I found myself spending a lot of time walking and driving aimlessly, seeking distraction and avoidance. One day, I drove with no particular destination in mind, and I couldn't bring myself to go to the studio and face Lauren. I knew she would see the panic in my face. Instead, I drove in circles from village to village until I stumbled upon a discreet farmer's track overlooking the Langley Park valley. I parked my van, left the engine running, but pulled the handbrake before breaking down in tears. I called my mam in Australia, who was with her friend at the time. She could tell right away that something was wrong, but I couldn't find the words to explain. All I managed to say was, 'It's messed up.' My mam couldn't do much from across the globe, but she offered words of comfort, emphasising the importance of family and suggesting that I needed to be strong for my daughters. While her words were kind and expected from a mother seeing her son in distress, they didn't provide the answers I needed or the £10,000 to resolve my immediate problem. As she hung up, I sat in the van, gripping the handbrake, contemplating letting go and allowing the van to roll down the track and over the edge into the valley. But deep down, I didn't want to die; I couldn't go through with it.

I eventually drove to another remote location and sent a text to my sister Lauren, who was working in the studio, unaware of my whereabouts or what I was going through. In that text, I told her, in no uncertain terms, that everything was a mess. She asked where I was, sensing my turmoil. When she found me, she got into the van, hugged me, and I began pouring out the whole truth for the first time. I felt like the world's biggest failure, ashamed and embarrassed. I couldn't protect her anymore or hide the reality that the business was failing. I confessed about the debt, our inability to trade our way out of the pandemic, and that the Clinkards opportunity was our last hope. Despite my previous declarations of optimism, Lauren wasn't naive; she could see we weren't busy. Through tear-filled eyes, I acknowledged that I couldn't promise her many more paydays. I apologised repeatedly and told her that I had failed. She responded with unwavering support, comforting me and assuring me that we were in this together, and we'd keep going as long as we could. Her compassion was enough to put a stop to the negative thoughts that had been consuming me.

It didn't take much longer for the inevitable to happen. Lauren and I were in the studio when she informed me that she needed to talk. I knew instantly what it was. She was leaving. My mental health was fragile, but I had to be strong at that moment. It wasn't Lauren's fault, and I needed to accept it with grace and dignity. Lauren had been an incredible colleague and supporter over the years we had worked together, and it was only right that she prioritised her own well-being. There were no tears, no emotional breakdowns. Instead, we shared a heartfelt hug, expressed our gratitude for each other, and agreed on her notice period. Her official departure date was set for 22nd December 2021, but not before one of the most peculiar situations I had ever encountered.

I received an email from a local church seeking volunteers for their choir. I initially drafted an email to decline the offer, injecting some humour about my complete inability to sing in tune. I composed the message in full, ready to hit the send button. However, in a decisive moment, I did something unexpected. I deleted every word I had written and changed my response. I accepted the invitation.

At that moment, I recognised that this decision would be something I'd look back on with pride. I couldn't think of a more effective way to step out of my comfort zone than singing in front of a live audience. While I wasn't particularly eager to join a choir, I also didn't want to become the kind of person who avoided discomfort by declining new challenges.

Fear, I reflected, is an intriguing emotion. I might not enjoy flying, yet I've boarded many aeroplanes in my life and plan to continue doing so. I would even consider skydiving if the opportunity presented itself. My greatest fear, it occurred to me, was being held back by fear itself. Fear can be exhilarating. When I experience fear, I often attempt to apply logic to the situation. Take skydiving, for instance. Do I want to do it? Yes, it would be a cool experience. Can it be done? Well, there's a process: a briefing, boarding the plane, jumping out with an experienced professional, and landing safely. I can say I've jumped out of a plane for the rest of my life. So, can I do it? Yes, I can, even if it's scary.

Now, singing is a different challenge. I'm not a great singer, but I can open my mouth and make sounds. Would I want to sing in a choir? It would be a unique experience to say I once sang in a choir. What's required? Simply replying to an email with a 'yes.' Then, I show up, listen to the choir coach, open my mouth, produce some sounds, and follow the tune of the song. Afterwards, I receive applause, and for the rest of my life, I can proudly say I once sang in a choir.

That's why I hit the delete button. Despite feeling at my lowest, the part of me that believes I can overcome anything still existed within. My inner resilience and determination were still present. I'm very proud of this achievement because it took a lot of guts - and I don't mean for the singing.

The following weeks were isolating. I had tried to convince myself that Lauren's departure was a positive development, as it would free up her salary to provide more flexibility and a chance to reset. However, each evening felt like the longest day, and every morning marked the beginning of another gloomy day. Trade remained slow, and when the shop fitters called again, I reluctantly paid the bill using my credit card. I was astonished that the transaction went through, and it left me feeling sick.

Chapter 16

The End

23rd December 2021. I don't know if it was rock bottom. I hope it was because I never want to be there again. You hear that phrase a lot when people talk about mental health. All I can say for sure is that on that day, I came closer than ever to ending my life. I'm not proud of this, but I can't be more honest than to say it as coldly and bluntly as that. I look back on it today with very mixed emotions. The pain I felt as I lay on my studio floor was crippling, and while I have had difficult days since and times when I have thought about suicide, nothing has ever felt as catastrophic as 23rd December 2021. It was pure despair, the likes of which I've not felt in the same magnitude since. Everything that I've talked about in this story so far pales into insignificance. My childhood. My journalism. OSC. Sofa Workshop. The resilience I found to overcome my mistakes with Maria and Lorenzo. It was all for nothing. I was a failure, and I felt far closer to the person I hated in my early twenties than the inspirational, glass-half-full champion I had professed to be in recent years.

My religious beliefs have never been particularly strong. I've had times in my life when I've gone to church, especially when I found myself in times of difficulty; I've prayed. I walked into a church once during my twenties, taking a seat at the back while the service played out. My grandad, who we called Duck-Duck Grandad because he lived by a river in the Norfolk Broads when I was a toddler, was a born-again Christian, and I grew up idolising him and my Duck-Duck Nana. Both he and my nana would take us to church whenever we visited. They took it very seriously. Their home was full of Bibles and crosses on the walls. There were pictures of Jesus and the only thing that was ever on TV was a religious film, particularly around Easter. Grandad would often tell the story of how Jesus saved him. He told me many times when he was alive that Christianity is in me, and that sometime in my life, I'd see it. I stood up in his church as a young child and found myself reading out an extract from the Bible to the congregation. He used to tell me that at that moment, he knew I was in safe hands. He hated tattoos and didn't like alcohol. He was an old-school Yorkshireman who, for as long as I'd known him, dedicated himself to one thing: God. He and Nana were born again in 1986. I was one year old at the time. The story he told me was of a postman who intercepted my grandad's depression as he found himself in a low period following the breakdown of his second marriage. The postman told him he should go to church and ask for help from Jesus, which he did. From that moment, everything changed for him. He remarried my Nana, and for the next three decades, he never looked back. He never let life's pressures get him down after that. He took most things in his stride and dedicated his life to helping others, specifically disabled people. In my teens, he was living in Salisbury and was a warden within a social housing association for disabled people. In his spare time, he would use his engineering and mechanical skills to dismantle old wheelchairs and make one good one from two broken ones. He bought the chairs out of his own money. Once they were fixed, he hired a lorry and drove to Tirana in Albania, all the way through Europe, distributing the chairs to the children living in poverty and suffering. He did this every year for around six years in a row. I visited Grandad shortly before he died, and he was showing me his computer. He'd built it himself from scratch and was very proud of how speedy the processor was. He spent almost an hour showing me the flight simulator he had perfected, flying me from Heathrow to southern France in a Boeing 717 via the joystick controller he had professionally set up. He could play the organ to a great standard. He was an able photographer. He was a handy carpenter, and he could strip a car down to its last bolt and then rebuild it again. He was, for me, the epitome of success. I once unwittingly saw a cheque he'd written out in his house for a local charity for a sum of £350. He never owned his own home, drove a decent car, or bought expensive things. He gave his money away to local Christian causes. I envied him sometimes. He was my hero. And so, it's easy to see why I've always had an attraction to Christianity and faith as a potential solution to my problems. It worked for him, and there is no man on the planet I look up to more than my grandad, so it often felt like a matter of time before I had my meet and greet with The Lord himself.

The reality is, however, that as much as I find it hard to admit because of my loyalty to Grandad, I know that I am an atheist. I've tried to embrace the idea of God and particularly Jesus, but the issue I have on the topic is that I believe that when people are searching, quite often, eventually, they'll find an answer, and for me, that's what happened with my grandad. I think he needed faith to be able to make a change in his life. I'm grateful he found Jesus because the lessons he brought me throughout my life, often lessons from the Bible, have been invaluable, and the pride I feel for what he did with his is truly unexplainable. My values are very Christian, but they have little to do with the faith. I see being born again as a focus for change, similar to someone finding exercise or mindfulness as a coping mechanism. Others find nutrition. Some find travel or new relationships, spirituality or cults. It goes the other way too when it comes to seeking more meaning or a sense of belonging. People change by choosing a new life in crime, alcohol or drugs. I hope I'm wrong about religion, that there is some almighty afterlife, and that my grandad is truly watching down on me as I write this book. I find it difficult to write about being an atheist because I feel like I'm being disrespectful of my grandad's lessons and faith. In my heart, I hope. But in my head, I don't think it's real, and my truth is that my grandad has had his life, a beautiful one, and he lives on in me and the rest of my family. Perhaps that is Heaven.

On 23rd December 2021, there was no Jesus moment, no matter how much I prayed. I was desperate for that touch on my shoulder, or for the room to light up like so many of the Christian stories I've heard throughout my life. As I gripped the chair, I begged for Jesus' help. My heart could not have been more open. But it didn't come. There was no story I could share with you, no matter how much I craved my grandad's faith to be true.

While he wouldn't thank me for comparing him to some almighty superpower, Neville Rodgers became the saviour I was yearning for that afternoon. Had he not ignored my plea for him not to arrive at my studio that afternoon, and had he not been there for me the way he was, reassuring me with his personal story in such a humble and dignified manner, who knows how I would have recovered?

My grandad would have undoubtedly said Neville's arrival was a gift from God, and he'd be upset with me for turning my back on the sign; I'm sure of it. Perhaps, one day, I'll understand.

Atheism has played its part in the ongoing battle with my own mind when it comes to suicidal ideology. In those darkest thoughts, the lack of a Heaven has become a reason to simply stay alive! There was some anger in my gut during the crisis that day. I wanted the pain to end, but the reality of the fact that I think death is terminal made the step away from that chair feel immensely heavier.

To this day, I have struggled to express and summarise what was going on in my mind on that winter's day, and a few more times since. I feel like it's undignified and ugly to use the word suicidal to describe my mindset. I feel like using such a catastrophic word as suicidal to describe my woe is an insult to the 800,000+ people who end their lives every year. I've had many conversations with my doctor and mental health professionals about the burden I feel using the word. At what point does a person become suicidal? Is it the thought that defines the illness? Is it the action? Is it the feeling? Do I need to have taken action to earn the right to say I was suicidal? What I know is that on that day, I could see the cliff, but I don't think I ever walked towards the edge. I couldn't. I didn't want to die. I just wanted it to end, and so, had Neville not arrived, I'm not convinced I would have taken that step which in my mind would have made me suicidal. I've never been suicidal - I have thought about ending my life many times, but thankfully, I've never crossed that line.

This disconnection with the word suicide has been one of the most difficult things for me to process since the event. I have found it hard to express how low I was feeling or to emphasise the severity of my depressive state without becoming embodied within the suicidal category. The only way I can sum up my mental health during the hopelessness of that day is that I wanted it to end, and until Neville's interjection, I didn't understand that there was any other way. It was those thoughts that were urging me to consider the most drastic of choices. Had I not reached out to Lauren, the only other option for me that day was to simply lie there for the rest of eternity, hoping it would go away. We all know that sweeping it under the carpet is equally never truly a choice, so it boiled down to a simple choice of two. Life or death.

I suspect it is this conundrum that sadly, many people misunderstand when they are told there is always a way. It is the lack of a pathway that closes the door and why in so many tragic cases, people choose the latter option, taking their own lives. A 50/50 choice is a scary place when the stakes are that high. When there is no obvious hope.

When Neville said those words to me that afternoon, I didn't understand how everything would be okay, but I trusted him. I had to. The other side of the coin wasn't an option. He, at that moment, became the role model I needed to begin my recovery.

Chapter 17

Liquidation

We had Christmas. It was a Christmas that couldn't have been more different from 2018 when I flew Mam over to the UK to join us. Neville had told us to enjoy Christmas, and he said that we would meet in January to work out the plan and decide how we would move forward, but even though I knew there was a plan forthcoming, it didn't take the worry away. How could it?

New Year's Day 2022 was the second-worst moment of my life. The worry had taken its toll on me over the festive period. Even today, I don't fully recall any memories from that Christmas other than the turmoil I was experiencing. I couldn't take any joy from anything, no matter how much I tried to tell myself that I should. The kids opening their presents passed me by. I spent some time in the pub, blocking out the stress by pretending it wasn't real, all too aware that come the turn of the year, it was all going to come rushing back.

We had invited some friends to stay with us over New Year. Historically, my relationship with alcohol had generally been quite positive. I consider myself a happy drinker, and nothing is more uplifting for me than spending time with my friends and family. But this day was different. We started drinking around lunchtime, heading to the local pub in the afternoon. Our friends, Chris and Mary - my voice of reason - knew I wasn't okay, but I played down the intensity of the situation. I didn't want to talk about it. I wanted to enjoy their company, and my depressing thoughts were too heavy to deal with.

As the day went on, it was like any other day. Drinks were flowing, the kids were all playing, and I cooked us all a homemade curry. The evening progressed, and suddenly it was midnight. Everyone had gone to bed, apart from me. Now I was alone with my thoughts, and this time, I had a belly full of courage. I continued to drink. I was pouring triple measures of rum with just a splash of coke. I don't know how many I had, but there were several. With every drink, I was asking myself if it was enough to end things. As I reached the bottom of the glass, inevitably I'd tell myself, 'One more,' which I duly served up.

It got to about 2:00 am, and I found myself writing a post on social media, sharing a somewhat disturbing teary photo alongside a desperate plea for help. I wrote;

I am writing this drunk. Sorry.

For around the last 3 days I've drafted several

New Year's poetic and powerful stories. About how 2021 had taught me XYZ. I couldn't hit the share button because it felt so contrived and unauthentic.

Truthfully, 2021 has been the hardest year of my life. In years gone by my biggest fear had been being stuck in a job I didn't want to be in. In 2021 it has been fear of losing the job I love more than almost anything. That has been tough.

So, the most authentic and honest thing I can post is a very real photo of what it has been like to be a business owner in 2021. I love my job so much. It is not about money. I want to share an honest portrayal of what small business means in 2021. It is heartbreak. Fear. Uncertainty. If this means you won't buy from me I understand but at least I can say I have been true.

So. Perhaps it's taken booze to post this. But. If nothing else. At least it is a) spelt correctly and b) honest.

Here's to 2022. I love you.

I regret posting that. It wasn't nice. I don't know what I expected, but what I hoped for was a miracle. I was hoping for another Neville.

Almost within minutes, Lauren walked into the living room after a few people tipped her off about the post. She took the rum away and cuddled into me, saying very little. She was out of words. I wasn't able to talk. I just wept into her shoulder. Shortly after, Mary joined us, which, if I'm honest, I wanted to happen. I wanted her to see me like this because I felt like I needed all the help I could get. I sobered up almost immediately as the magnitude and adrenaline kicked in. I opened up and told Mary everything. The director's loan. The shop fitters' invoice. The lack of trade. Credit cards. I told her, all in all, it was about £125,000 worth of debt, most of which I'd personally guaranteed. She was taken aback. She didn't quite realise the enormity of it and referred back to the champagne celebrations she had seen on social media only weeks before, assuming things were on the up. 'This is the thing with business; sometimes', Lauren explained on my behalf. 'We have to pretend it's all going well; otherwise, nobody will buy anything from you. So, your social media content and your email marketing are more often than not an ill-informed version of reality. It is about what you do so well and how fantastic your brand is doing, and yet, the one thing social media doesn't share is your revenue, or more importantly, your profit.' It was hard to open up about the severity of it all beyond Lauren, but I felt like it needed to happen.

I've thought a lot since both times when I found myself

feeling desperately low and considering suicide as a real option. Arguably the largest contributing factor to the demise was the sense of failure. I was quite simply devastated. As I explained earlier, I live my life the majority of the time as a glass-half-full type. I get my kicks from helping others believe more in themselves. I'm from a working-class background, as I've explained, and as a family, we didn't have a great deal of luxuries growing up, but that's never stopped me from believing that my destiny was far greater than the one I was perceived to be heading for as a young man. I wanted this, more than anything, to be my legacy. Every day that I woke up knowing I was a business owner, I was closer to creating this legacy. Simon Bourne, the boy from Scunthorpe who had an idea and changed his life. I desperately wanted that message for my children. I wanted my school friends to hear about me, and my school to put my face on the wall as inspiration for young kids.

Was 2019 the greatest year of my life because of trade and revenues, or was it because of the attention I was getting? I am, after all, a seeker of attention. I was so desperate for accolades that I couldn't see anything in front of me beyond failure, greed, narcissism, manipulation, ego, and selfishness. I was a liar and a cheat. I'd conned everyone, including my friends and my family, into believing I was going to be something special. I'd led my wife and children into believing I was an entrepreneur and that my decisions to take loans and sign personal guarantees would pay off. I wasn't an entrepreneur. I was a fraud.

Lauren took my phone and deleted the post. I am pleased she did. Soon after, we all retired safely to bed. By morning, Mary insisted I should call the doctors to make an appointment. I was somewhat dismissive of the idea. I had a predetermined opinion about medication, and I felt somehow that succumbing to tablets was in some way another failure. It was a failure of my personality. I wasn't able to be the glass-half-full guy if I medicated. The idea of it somehow made me even more of a fraud. Nevertheless, I trusted her like a sister, and given her profession as a mental health nurse, I didn't have much choice other than to listen to her. I made an appointment.

We had agreed to meet with Neville on the 6th January 2022. I told Neville we would come to his office in Sunderland. I was struggling to face my studio given where I was mentally and how I'd felt the last day I was in there. Lauren came with me. I needed her there for comfort but also for a second opinion on whatever advice we were about to get. I didn't want to have to relay the message; I wasn't sure I could.

As we arrived, Neville made us coffee, and we pulled up a chair. I'd brought along my laptop, and one of the first things we did was open up the accounts. I felt a little awkward, given that Neville had spent a lot of money with me over the years and was now privy to how much profit I'd made from him. We were operating, at our peak, at around 57% gross profit which when we were trading close to 100 pairs per month, made for a very tidy net profit at the end of it. Of course, we had creditors to pay, and with the recruitment of Lauren and Laura, the wages meant we were pretty much in line to break even month-by-month had trade continued at pre-Covid rates. I was comfortable with that at the time I took the loans because it was a means to an end. We could lose money for a while whilst we built the team and honed in on our marketing messages.

It didn't take Neville long, though, to condemn what he was looking at. The director's loan. The creditors. The level of trade. He knew I couldn't pull it back. I knew it, and Lauren knew it too. However, until now, I didn't understand that there was any other way.

'You need to liquidate your company,' he said.

It was a word I'd heard before but didn't know what it meant. As an avid football fan, over the years, I've read many times about clubs going into liquidation. I'd also read about administration and receivership. Then there were winding-up orders and insolvency. It was all another language to me. I didn't know if it was all the same thing or not. No matter, I still felt like I had a bowling ball in my stomach the moment he said the words. 'What will happen to the brand?' I gingerly asked. When you liquidate a company, you can either do it yourself or you can do it via a registered insolvency practitioner. If you do it yourself, this is called voluntary liquidation. The idea of volunteering didn't sit well with Lauren or me because we felt there were too many elements that would be left open. We needed some closure. So our preferred method was to liquidate through a practitioner. The problem with that, though, is that the practitioners would expect to be paid for the privilege, and it doesn't take a genius to work out that we had no money.

Neville went on. 'What the practitioner will do,' he explained, 'they'll value your assets and essentially sell off what they can. Whatever they can raise, they'll pay themselves their fee, and anything else beyond that they'll use to pay your creditors. If they can't raise enough to pay back your creditors in full, they'll look to do a deal with them based on a split of the remaining balance they could raise.' It sounded perfect. Fantastic. But the problem I had was that my business had very few assets. We didn't own a property or have any large value items on our balance sheet. We were largely made up of sample shoes - which were either a left or a right foot because we never needed two the same for samples - and therefore they had little value too. I could only make a case for around £1,000 worth of assets.

It was an intense couple of hours. By the end of the

meeting, we agreed to adjourn and meet again alongside a licensed insolvency practitioner so that we could establish the facts about the best route forward. Neville made two calls. The first was to a practitioner in Newcastle. He arranged a meeting for the 10th January 2022, which, unbeknown to Neville, was my birthday. The second call was to Peter Gray, a retired practitioner whom Neville had dealt with in the past.

The morning of my birthday came. There was little time for sentiment, or interest if I'm honest. Lauren and I drove back to Sunderland and met with Neville and Peter at 10.00 am. I'm not sure what I expected, but Peter Gray wasn't the image of a man I'd rest my life in the hands of. He wore a black and grey pinstripe suit. It looked like something from Miami Vice or some American lawyer-type movie. He had long black hair, tied back in a ponytail. His shoes were, well, black. His accent was thick Geordie. He was from Gateshead and whilst my accent is distinctively northern, Peter's was about as northern as it gets.

Neville took the lead, explaining the situation to Peter. All of a sudden, it was like someone had plugged him in. He took off like a cat stalking its prey.

'Firstly, I'm retired, and I don't have a licence to practice now,' he said. 'Plus, I don't want any money from this. Listen carefully. Here's what we will do. We will liquidate the company. If you can find a buyer for your few assets and the intellectual property that your company, Hand Dyed Shoe Co. Ltd., does have, then that could give you the funds to pay the liquidator. Whoever buys those assets and intellectual property can then use it to set up a new company which can trade as Hand Dyed Shoe Company - given that the name, logo, website, and trademarks all form part of the intellectual property.'

I was deeply confused. I was scared. So was Lauren. It didn't sound legal. How could this be right?

Peter put a rough figure of £6,000 on what a practitioner would be looking for in order to liquidate Hand Dyed Shoe Co. Ltd. Neville offered to buy the assets and intellectual property, but he would not be willing to pay that much. I delved deeper into it.

'If the practitioner wants £6,000, and let's just say we can raise that figure by selling the assets and intellectual property, what will happen to the rest of the debt?' At this point, we owed Funding Circle around £56,000.

'It will just go,' Peter shrugged. What will happen is this: The practitioner will take the £6,000 fee for their services. They'll write to all the companies that you owe money to and tell them that they've taken ownership of Hand Dyed Shoe Co. They'll invite your creditors to a consultation where they'll tell them what funds they've been able to raise for the pot, which unfortunately for them, will be nothing beyond the £6,000 the practitioner is due.'

'What will happen to my director's loan?' I asked.

'Yes, that will be a problem. Because you owe Hand Dyed Shoe Co. Ltd. almost £27,000. So, they will also write to you and ask you to pay that money into the pot.'

'But, we don't have £27,000,' I declared. 'And why would Funding Circle care about the pot when I have signed a personal guarantee?'

'If you don't have the funds, then you only have one option,' he said.

'Bankruptcy.'

Chapter 18

The Loss

I fell silent. I could feel the pulse in my neck beating against the inside of my skin. My palms were sweating, and the blood vessels in my wrists were swollen. I felt stunned, frozen in my seat. India. Journalism. The Bvlgari Hotel. Sofa Workshop. My entire working life. It was all for nothing. My heart was broken, and our family was broken. Everything was gone. Our home. Vanilla. Our family cars. Our television. The children's toys. Everything we had ever worked for. We were quite literally broke, and it was my fault.

I didn't know what bankruptcy meant, in truth. I was basing this entire theory on assumption. I had no prior experience or understanding of the process and wasn't aware of anybody I knew who had been through the process. Peter began painting the picture. When you go bankrupt, you can't be a director for 12 months, so you'd have to get a job. However, if someone buys your assets and intellectual property and use that property to trade under another company, you can be employed by it. The process is almost identical to that when you liquidate a company. You liquidate a company because it is insolvent. You bankrupt a human because he or she is insolvent. Insolvent, in simple terms, means that you can't afford to pay your creditors.'

I was beginning to process. I was grateful Lauren was sitting beside me, even though it made my stomach churn knowing she was hearing the same torment as I was. Peter continued. When you file for bankruptcy, your personal assets will form part of your personal estate. You will be assigned an Insolvency Practitioner, known as an Official Receiver, and that person will be charged with assessing your application. Their job is to fill the pot to pay your personal creditors, just the same as the Insolvency Practitioner is in charge of filling a pot to pay your business creditors.'

My mind was immediately on our home. I owned our home 50-50 with Lauren. Peter explained that the good news in all of this was that Lauren was not liable for any of the debt as she was not a director of the company, nor did she have any involvement with the credit agreements I'd signed. That meant that she was not liable to repay anything I'd borrowed, and neither the Insolvency Practitioner nor the Official Receiver could enforce anything on her assets.

'The Insolvency Service will have an interest in your vehicle and any equity that you have in your property,' Peter reassuringly told us. 'It's unlikely that they will have any interest in anything else you own, given there is nothing of significant value. They can't enforce any interest in anything that belongs to Lauren or the children.'

That was the line I needed to hear. I was visibly emotional but was able to maintain some control and dignity as Peter went into the details. 'It's unlikely that they would enforce a house sale,' he said. 'To ascertain an eviction, the Insolvency Service would have to find you new accommodation, and with two children and an innocent partner, alongside up-to-date mortgage payments, it's highly unlikely that a court would support an eviction. That will leave two scenarios. They could apply to put a charge on your property, which would be decided based on the valuation of your estate, and you will have to add the charge to the mortgage balance. The third option would be that you agree to a deal with the service where you, in essence, buy back the financial interest in the property with a cash lump sum.'

All three scenarios were drastically frightening. But we felt reassured that there was potential that we wouldn't lose everything and that while the consequences were going to be difficult and uncomfortable, there was a way we could negotiate our way through this difficult path ahead. Somehow, we might be able to rebuild from a significantly better place than I initially thought.

Bankruptcy was, without a doubt, going to be a long and

difficult journey, but it offered a huge incentive. It offered closure to the nightmare. It meant that the debt phone calls would stop. The director's loan, HMRC, Funding Circle, credit cards, it would all be gone from my mind, and I could be free.

The consequences were uncertain, but seemingly from Peter's experience, the road was rocky but not undrivable. I felt a weird moment of encouragement. Arguably excitement. I recognised the feeling. It wasn't one I'd felt for some time, probably since Covid first began. It was that sense of adventure. The feeling I had when I went to Portugal over those two days. I had a job to do, but instead of a Porsche staring back at me from the horizon, instead, it was peace.

I was very confused emotionally and fairly exhausted by the time Peter left, and we drove up to our second meeting with the Insolvency Practice. The good thing was, it was a fairly quick meeting. I didn't let on that I'd already had some advice. I just used my new armour of knowledge to challenge the process and their understanding of what I should do. Luckily for us, as I embarked on the story for the second time that day to a complete stranger, the feedback was pretty much identical. They quoted me £6,500 to liquidate Hand Dyed Shoe Co. Ltd. Neville pushed back, suggesting he would be willing to pay them £2,000 for the assets and intellectual property. We couldn't reach a deal there and then, so eventually we all left.

Lauren and I hugged Neville before we went our separate ways. We didn't plan another meeting. We just agreed to take some time and pick up when we were ready. There was so much to take in.

I visited my doctor soon after. It was one of the most difficult conversations I've ever had. I consider myself to be quite good at talking about my emotions and feelings, particularly with Lauren, but for some reason, the doctor's waiting room was all I needed to lose control of myself. As I sat waiting to be called, I was visibly shaking. Tears were strolling down my face before I'd even said a word. The doctor came out and called my name. I scurried to her room and took a seat. I don't think I spoke for the first five minutes. I just cried. Eventually, when I started to explain things, the suicidal thoughts, the stress, anxiety, depression. I spoke through a broken voice, and I recall asking the doctor several times if I was suicidal. I don't know why it mattered to have the label or not. I still don't know now. I asked her what would happen if I had attempted suicide. I wanted her to know how intense things were in my brain at that moment, and I feared that perhaps I wouldn't get taken seriously unless I told her I had attempted to harm myself. I challenged her on the differences between depression, anxiety, and stress. I needed to know what this was. I needed to know which label I was dealing with. I was overthinking it all but felt reassured by her answer. Depression is clinical. It's deeper, usually long-term, and it is often accompanied by a feeling of emptiness and hopelessness. Anxiety is an inner feeling of worry that doesn't go away, even when your stress factors aren't triggering. Stress is more of a reaction. It presents itself often as a state of anger or panic.

The doctor defined my symptoms as anxiety, but I'm not so sure. I have come to understand that what I suffer from, and have suffered from largely throughout my life, is an inability to deal with intense stress. I am hyperactive and full of energy most of the time, but at the same time, I'm also very calm, laid-back, and simplistic. I have often used the word lazy to describe that side of me during the low periods when I'm not being kind to myself. Stress in me is often initiated when these natural characteristics are disturbed, and it presents itself as overthinking, panic, and self-sabotage. I can easily sink into intense questioning during periods of stress where I spiral around and around, questioning and answering within my brain. If I sleep too long, I spend a significant amount of time trying to work out what that means. Often, the conclusion is negative. I'm lazy. If I lose my temper and shout, it is because I didn't feel loved as a child. I'd think often about mental health and the advice that is out there. I should talk. Open up. But, if I open up, at what point am I asking for help, and at what point am I being pathetic and wallowing in self-pity? I should walk and connect with nature. But at what point do I understand why

I'm doing it because when I do, all I'm doing is walking. I should be in the moment; find value in the moment I'm in right now. But how could I do that when the moment I was in right now was suffocated with debt? There were no other moments. It was all I could think about when I was cooking, and taking the girls to a park. Even during intimacy, I was thinking about how this could well be the last time I made love with my wife.

Perhaps I was suffering from anxiety - this wasn't a new feeling, after all. I'd never had these feelings with such intensity as I was feeling right then, but they weren't new feelings. The doctor concluded that Sertraline, an antidepressant tablet, would be the best solution to help me regulate my mood and reduce anxiety. She also recommended I self-refer for Cognitive Behavioural Therapy, which I agreed to do. The last thing she recommended was to write things down. 'Put a journal beside your pillow, and just scribble things down. When you wake up in the night, before you sleep, just jot down how you are feeling and then use it to provoke discussions with Lauren.' I also agreed to try this.

I called Peter and told him I needed to find £6,000 to liquidate Hand Dyed Shoe Co. Ltd. I told him Neville would be willing to pay £2,000. I wasn't awake enough to understand or consider the game at that moment, but Neville was clearly negotiating. For his negotiation tactic to be successful, though, it would require time, and for me, I didn't have time. I just needed closure, as soon as possible so that I could begin to move on and resolve my anxiety and stress. Peter said he'd make some calls to some other practitioners he knew from throughout his career, and he'd explain the situation to them on my behalf. Within an hour, he called me back and told me that he knew a company that would be willing to liquidate the company for £4,500. That felt more achievable.

With Neville's £2,000 and the £3,500 I'd raised from selling my car, I instructed the Insolvency Practitioner to start the process and make sure the kids had what they needed for a few more weeks, at least.

The tattoo on my arm is part of a sleeve which also bears a portrait of Daisy. It's no coincidence that these two important aspects of my life shared the same bit of skin. They were very much on par with one another in terms of how much they meant to me, which probably tells you why I was so distraught about the whole collapse. I meant what I said earlier. The tattoo had so much more sentiment than shoes. But right now, at this moment, it felt stupid. It was a reminder of naivety and arrogance, as opposed to joy. Liquidating my business, my company, felt as painful as death. It was, in a sense, the death of me.

Chapter 19

Born Again

Lauren and I were both feeling exceptionally vulnerable, and my thinking was very erratic. I was going from one idea to the next with regard to what I should do. Should I work with Neville and be a part of his new company? Maybe I should start applying for jobs. I found myself in turmoil with the decision, quite often in the early hours of the morning. I wanted the brand to continue, desperately. *But would I feel the same emotions and passion for it without my name above the door? How would I feel working for someone else who owned my brand? It was my baby. And if anyone was going to own my brand, did I want it to be Neville?*

Neville had saved me from my studio floor just a few months before. He'd got me to this position by holding my hand through the difficult conversations and by offering the olive branch in terms of his finances. He was willing to save the brand and give me a second chance. But, at what cost?

I'm far from proud that I questioned his motives, but I did. I think it would have been foolish not to ask myself those questions. *What if Neville was somehow trying to cap-*

italise on me? Was he trying to take ownership of my brand knowing that it was the potential gold mine that I wasn't able to create? Was he interested in the Clinkards' relationship? Why would he help me? What's in it for him? These were all thoughts that were going through my head as I approached the day when we were going to create the new company, and he was going to buy the assets and intellectual property. I was scared. I'd already been through so much torture, I couldn't face being taken advantage of and perhaps making the situation worse than it already was. I talked it over with friends, and there was a lot of scepticism. There was a fairly unanimous conclusion that people don't do these things for nothing, and therefore, there must be more to Neville's offering than simple kindness. Fear took hold.

Lauren and I travelled through to Sunderland to meet Neville. He assumed we were coming to finalise the paperwork and sort the legalities. I was so nervous. I wasn't sure if I was doing the right thing or not. As I sat down, Neville made us coffee, and I started. The opening line was the single worst sentence that has ever come out of my mouth. 'Neville, we can't go ahead with the new business.' He looked stunned. The reason it was the worst line was I had basically just told him that my mind was made up. I wasn't even going to allow him to talk me down or reason with me. I was desperately apologetic. He was visibly angry, yet it didn't spill over into anything beyond a few expressions of disappointment. I tried to somewhat backtrack after seeing his reaction, which was cowardly if anything. I told him I needed to be sure and that I needed time to decide if this was the right thing to do. We weren't there long. I left, and as I got in my van, I felt like the most disgusting human being on the planet. I had just told the man who dragged me out of the dirt I didn't trust him. I messed up.

I tried to reconcile the situation, but the next day, Neville called me and said he wasn't my guy and that he was hurt by my mistrust. He had shared a lot of his vulnerabilities with me and shared his personal story, so for me to question his trust was a step too far. I was ashamed of myself, but I didn't have time to wallow. I needed to take action. Not only had I just lost a relationship, but I'd now also lost the £2,000 I needed to liquidate the business. I needed options, quickly.

I met up with David Robinson, my old boss at The Original Sofa Company. He had been through similar financial difficulties, and I felt like he could potentially help me with his experience, which he did. He seemed interested in what I'd achieved, and he too offered to get involved. I trusted David, even if I didn't enjoy the scatty way he ran his businesses. In the end, he was indecisive as to whether there was a deal to be done. Too much time passed, and with each day came more debt letters and phone calls, leaving me feeling more desperate to get things moving than ever.

I had one more option. I'd known Bill Turner for over 20 years. He was a friend of the family, and I was sure I could trust him. He'd been in business before and had been successful both professionally and entrepreneurially. I met him in the local pub and explained the predicament I was in. I sold it to him that all it would cost was £2,000. He becomes the owner of the assets and intellectual property, and he owns the company. He would then employ me to run the business from an operational point of view. I'd make sure there were enough sales, and all he has to do is make sure I get paid my salary. The Leeds relationship was still intact, and Clinkards was still on board with the collaboration - there was potential that that could grow. Any profit the company would make, it's free money for him. He was on board.

I'd worked out that for me to make my salary, I needed to sell around 18 pairs of shoes. Even post-COVID, we were doing 20-25 on average, so I felt like it was attainable, and if nothing else, it would buy me time to make some more permanent decisions about my future.

I'd said to Lauren several times that I wanted to walk away from the brand. I'd become so deeply embedded in this feeling of failure that my head wanted to quit, badly. I felt like I couldn't take any more of the stress and the pressure, and the guy who could once do anything had been proven wrong. I couldn't do business. I couldn't handle money. I couldn't inspire or create a winning team. It was much safer to get a job. The problem I had was I was in no fit state to search for employment, let alone apply for anything. I didn't feel I could attend an interview and sell myself. I couldn't fill in an application form. There were a few times I explored job websites, but each time I looked, I couldn't find anything that caught my attention or made me feel inspired. I didn't even know what to look for. I described myself to Lauren as unemployable because my mental health was so unstable, and I feared that doing a job for money or without love could make things even worse.

Lauren was adamant every time I mentioned walking away from the brand, even before I explained my reasoning. It had to continue. She knew how hard I'd worked, and she knew how much it had impacted my life both on a professional level and a personal one. I was a better husband when I was doing my own thing. Employment for me was always restrictive and fraught with insecurities. I didn't take criticism well. I didn't deal with authority particularly well. I questioned everything in the establishment, and what that meant about me. My boss at Sofa Workshop once told me I had an ego. That killed my spirit for weeks. I didn't think I had an ego. Far from it. I consider myself a humble person, and I considered the accusation to be a slander of my personality. I felt like I cared more about other people than I did myself, and I considered the word ego as self-centred and arrogant. I couldn't stop thinking about it, and to a degree, I still think about it today. I beat myself up about it and felt ugly. Egos are about power and greed. I've come to accept that egos are also about winning and competition. They're about being the best and enjoying the accolades and accomplishments of the success you strive for. I suspect my boss was probably angling slightly towards that side of the comment when she said it, but irrespective, it was a clear indication to me that employment was just too confusing for me, and I was better off answering to myself. Or, more to the point, answering to my wife. Lauren knows me better than anybody else on the planet. She can tell me how I'm feeling before I even know myself. She knows if I'm hurting before I've even opened my mouth. I don't even need to be with her. She can tell it from a text message or the lack of one. She understands how to pick me up and how to bring me down when I need that too. I credit Lauren with everything I've become. She was the first person I felt pure unconditional love from and where there were simply no boundaries to it. We've grown up together from teenagers into parents. At 18 years old, I got my first house - a council house within my local village. She came to stay the first night I moved in, and from that moment, she never left. She is far more cautious and risk-averse than I am; she offers balance and unwavering support to all my decision-making, even if she wouldn't have made the same decision. Throughout all the torment, she never once blamed me, suggested I'd made a mistake or looked back at any decisions with regret or remorse. She was unequivocally alongside me, and she cared only about one thing and one thing only: our family.

Cautious but adamant. She was insistent. 'You can't quit!'

I signed the paperwork and passed over ownership of the business to the Insolvency Practitioners on the 16th February 2022. I was no longer a business owner. A few days later, Bill paid the £2,000 to the practitioners, and I paid the rest from the money I raised from selling Vanilla. It was done.

Bill registered his company, FCC Retail Trading Ltd., with Companies House, and we seamlessly transferred the business assets and intellectual property over into his name. My customers, at this time, were unaware of any changes, and things continued as normal. All existing orders were delivered to protect the reputation of the brand, and all gift vouchers within the business were to be honoured by FCC. This meant that Bill's new company began life with a liability to Hand Dyed Shoe Co.'s customers. However, Bill and I agreed that if the brand was to survive, we had to make sure that the customers were looked after.

The brand was born again. It had no debt, other than to our customers. Overnight, we had gone from an operational cost of almost £25,000 per month to under £5,000. Ultimately, this meant we needed to sell a lot less to operate, and that, above everything else, allowed me to breathe.

Chapter 20

Closure

If there was one thing I wanted in my business from the start, it was a team. I never really wanted to be the sole director of my company, and over the years, I had many conversations with people about the idea of coming on board as a director. I always felt slightly under-equipped on the business side of things and often wished I had someone else there, with equal investment in the project on an emotional level, to help me push it forward and for accountability. Having someone else there who had ownership of the finances would have perhaps saved me from making the mistakes that had got me into this mess. For whatever reason, it never happened. I had plenty of offers from people who wanted to get involved, but never from anyone I felt entirely comfortable with. I found it difficult to trust people's motives and to be convinced of the value they could bring. The people I wanted to get involved with were either too busy with other projects or perhaps not convinced that mine was sustainable enough for them to achieve what they needed in life.

All of a sudden, I had a business partner, albeit, it was

no longer my business. I had a boss, and it wasn't simple. Bill is much older than me and much more old-school when it comes to how a business works. My approach is quite millennial. I'm driven by the feeling of making things happen. I can easily get through 100 tasks a day because I get a buzz out of juggling many different plates and making things happen. It's no coincidence that the business was created in the first place and I made that trip to Portugal. I was a runner, after all. Bill is very much the opposite. His preferences were very much geared towards writing things down and giving decisions a lot of thought. He likes to take his time. His communication skills were very different to mine. I am very open while Bill is very closed when it comes to sharing thoughts and ideas. He would generally prefer to say nothing and to take things slowly - often leaving me wondering what was happening. I felt my frustrations growing all of the time as I waited for him to pay an invoice or open a new business bank account.

Having assumed it would be a simple transition, I quickly realised that the simplicity of my working for him, under the umbrella of my brand and the functionality of the way I like things done, was going to be particularly difficult. It was, however, my punishment. I felt I had to accept it as part of my fate for messing up my company. This new existence wasn't going to be easy, but it was better than working for an establishment I didn't much care for. I had to let go of how I was feeling and I had to teach myself the art of patience. I had to consider Bill's world and the fact that out of nowhere, he was suddenly the owner of a business that he had not asked for and that he was operating within it outside of his day-to-day life, including his job. It wasn't going to be easy, but it was the best option I had available both personally and professionally.

That's how I sold it to myself, anyway, and how I was usually able to bring my emotions back into order when things were getting particularly arduous.

Aside from managing the new situation within the brand, I still had to process the routine calls from the likes of American Express, Funding Circle, HMRC, and other creditors. Soon after the liquidators had taken over Hand Dyed Shoe Co. Ltd., I started to receive calls from creditors' debt collection teams as they received the news that the business was now defunct. I never ignore a call. For me, ignoring the calls would have been me not taking responsibility, and while difficult, I am very much on the side of the fence of doing the right thing, rather than playing dirty. I figured that the best way of dealing with this situation was to speak with the companies and let them know the situation.

Of course, I knew that the most likely outcome here was that I was going to have to file for bankruptcy, which would mean that these companies wouldn't receive a great deal in terms of repayments. I explained this to each creditor as they called, hopeful that perhaps there may be another way, and that somehow I could avoid the headache and difficulty of having to wrestle with the Insolvency Service and the Official Receiver to keep a roof over my family's heads. I explained that my business had gone into liquidation and that I was aware of the personal guarantees I had signed. I explained that as things stand, I was now employed, but my salary was nowhere near enough to be able to cover the repayments.

Answering the calls was, without a doubt, the best decision I made. The vast majority of the creditors were understanding and kind. Funding Circle, particularly, I found to be empathetic and compassionate as I explained the turmoil that the collapse of my business was having on my mental health. I'd been warned by many people that these companies don't care and that they wouldn't think twice about making your life a living hell to get their money back. It wasn't the experience that I had. I found that if you talk, there is compassion from these teams. Of course, their agenda is to get their money back, but if there's nothing you can do, then there aren't many options available to them either, so I didn't feel there was any overwhelming threat. I promised to keep an open line of communication, and in return, they agreed to leave me alone for a period while I worked things out. I found this very helpful, and it removed the fears I had of someone knocking on my door and taking all of our belongings away.

As time went on, I was feeling closer and closer to having to make that bankruptcy decision. I felt an obligation to my creditors to bring the issue to a close because even though there were offers to flex repayments, extend terms, and pause agreements, I knew that closure was the only option. I needed a clean slate.

In total, there were around seven companies that I owed money to. None of the debts were household bills or personal loans; they were all related to the business. On the evening of the 25th April 2022, Lauren and I decided that the next morning, I would file for bankruptcy. I didn't feel like it was fair to keep asking for more time when, in reality, I couldn't foresee anything changing in the short term. As dawn broke, I took Daisy to school and dropped Penny at her grandma's. When I returned home, I called each of my creditors and spoke with the debt collection teams. I told them of my intention, and I apologised. I'm not naive enough to think that the person on the other end of the phone would have any bias or personal obligation to pass the message up the chain, but for me, it was about respect and doing the right thing. At the end of the day, all business is business. And while these businesses are humongous in size, largely operated by boardrooms, backed by huge pockets of investors, and my default was in the grand scheme of things, pennies, I felt obliged to place my apology on file because someone, somewhere, was going to be affected in some way, and when I took those loans, that was never my intention. I felt that if there was ever to be a future for me where a Porsche was within it, I owed it to the people who already drove Porsches to acknowledge their achievements. It was my way of putting into the universe, if you will, my dignity and honour.

Filling in the bankruptcy forms isn't a quick process. There are pages upon pages of questions about your existence and ultimately, why you are doing this. Of course, I was aware that everything I said was going to be scrutinised, and because of that, it made it extremely nerve-wracking. The form asks you about your creditors, how much you owe them, and some narrative around the circumstances. The hardest part, I found, was filling in the section where you declare your assets. Peter had told me that they wouldn't have any interest in things such as televisions or electrical goods. The children's belongings were safe, along with anything that belonged to Lauren. They would have an interest in any items worth £1,000 or more. I didn't own anything of that value, other than my van, my half of the equity within my home, and perhaps my camera. I didn't have any art collections or high-value jewellery.

At the end of completing the form, you submit the form, but not before paying the princely sum of £680 for the privilege. The irony is unfathomable.

Then, it was a case of waiting. It was such a strange thing to be waiting for. In one sense, I was waiting for a piece of paper which says that Simon Bourne was no longer liable for these debts and in more important terms, must be left alone. The risk of a bailiff or any more debt collection calls was over. On the other hand, it was the beginning of 12 months of new risks and new conversations. What lay ahead for me was worrying. *What if Peter had got it wrong, and they would seek an eviction? What will happen to my van? How will I get to work? What will my family think when they hear I've gone bankrupt? What about my friends? Old friends? School friends?* In the buildup to the day, I'd met up with a few people and told them what was going to happen. My friend, Helen, told me she had filed for bankruptcy some years before after her relationship failed and she was left with unaffordable debt. Helen is someone I admire greatly. She's a business owner herself and reassured me that whilst it's tough, the thick of it only lasts one year and after that, you're free to rebuild your life. She was a great example of why it was important that I lived. If Helen could come back from this and be a figurehead of success, I could come back from this too. It was reassuring. When we told Lauren's parents, it was a more difficult conversation. There is so much stigma around bankruptcy, particularly from the older generation. It was, historically, looked upon with shame. It was the rubber stamp of a person who had failed or neglected their finances. It was a gambler's punishment. Your family name would be published in the paper, telling the world you're bankrupt. These days, there's a register, and your name will appear amongst an endless public list of other people who have failed. There was clear discomfort, which didn't make things easier for me.

The thought of my name being publicly printed for the world to see that I was bankrupt wasn't something I was proud of. I find it a little bizarre, to be honest. The whole experience of being declared bankrupt is, I imagine, a very similar journey to that of a criminal. The threats are similar. Sex offenders are forced to sign a register and it is used in the media and law courts as a deterrent. This was the same punishment for my crime. My family name. My grandad's name. My wife's name. My children's name. My name. That was hard to bear. The judge - in this case, the Official Receiver - would determine my outcome and decide my fate.

Once I'd pressed the button and submitted my application for bankruptcy, I felt a huge breath leave my body. I made a cup of tea but it went cold before I drank it as my thoughts were heavily distracted. I knew from that moment, the risk of someone knocking on the door for a debt and my daughter's witnessing it was no longer there. I was feeling embarrassed, ashamed and very sorry, but nobody needed to know about it other than those who might find out by searching my name on the Insolvency Register. We could keep it to ourselves. It's private knowledge.

I was anticipating a call from the service to discuss my application. My understanding of the process is that someone would call to go through it and check all the facts and numbers in an interview. I wasn't anticipating it to be so quick. It was the next morning, bang on 9.00 am when the phone rang. I was getting dressed and immediately sat down in a chair and listened very carefully. My body was tense, but I was focused. I needed to be honest and I needed to keep it clean. I knew I had nothing to hide, but I didn't want to say anything that might cause us more problems as a family or jeopardise our chances of saving our family home. The stakes were as high as anything I'd ever risked before.

The call lasted for about an hour. The Official Receiver asked lots of questions and requested a lot of documentation. He asked me to send bank statements, the V5 log book for my van and the Vitesse I'd sold a few months ago. I had to share details about my camera and the lenses I owned. Any bank accounts I owned. I had to send copies of life insurance policies and mortgage details.

After I'd sent the documents, it was a case of waiting to see what happened next. The silence is, as they say, what kills you. The worry was intense, but all we could do was wait.

One of the first problems we had was that somewhat

out of the blue, my bank accounts were frozen. When we visited the bank, they said that they'd been instructed by the Insolvency Service to withhold any funds. Any money we did have in the bank was from both of our salaries. It was a desperate situation because all of a sudden, we had no access to any money and as you can imagine, with two children, we panicked about how long this might take to fix. The banks said that they needed instruction from the Insolvency Service to say that they held no interest in the funds, but for that to happen it needed to be reviewed by the service. As with most large organisations, these things don't happen quickly.

I contacted the Official Receiver and explained the predicament we were facing. He was understanding and assured me that he would send a letter confirming that they had no interest in our accounts. We patiently waited, and it arrived approximately 24 hours later. We printed it and rushed to the bank, but unfortunately, they couldn't accept it in person. I needed to reach out to a specialist team via telephone, who would then request the letter via email. It was an incredibly stressful day, filled with running around and trying to resolve the issue, and it took the entire day to finally have our accounts released.

As for other accounts with fewer funds, they presented a different problem. The banks simply closed these accounts. When I inquired about it, they explained that due to my bankruptcy, I was no longer entitled to that type of account.

Administratively, I hadn't considered these implications.

Soon after the interview, I received a letter from the service confirming my bankruptcy status:

> *Upon reviewing the application submitted on 26/04/2022, it is ordered that Mr. Simon David Bourne be declared bankrupt.*

This news brought about mixed feelings, but primarily it was one of relief. The daily deluge of phone calls and letters had ceased. The debt was no longer hanging over me. I was going to be okay. I had finally found some closure.

Chapter 21

Distraction

By this point, Bill had assumed full control of the new business, and the adjustment was still challenging for me. There were days when my frustration from not having control would spill over, and I'd find myself angrily questioning how Bill was running things. I recognised my petulance then, and I acknowledge it now. Whenever it became too much, Lauren would help calm me down. Overall, I was content, just barely. It was certainly better than the alternative of Hand Dyed Shoe Co. disappearing entirely. Bill and I agreed to meet monthly to discuss the business's status. I was comfortable with certain aspects, such as distancing myself from responsibilities like accounting and dealings with HMRC. Focusing solely on sales felt somewhat simpler, affording me time to address other aspects of my life, both logistical and mental. Selling 20 pairs of shoes a month was my target to maintain the stability of our household.

It was strange not to feel the pressure of needing to sell 100 pairs per month just to pay off creditors and staff. With no employees other than myself, I found I had a lot more free time. I began working from home more often, handling my emails and immediate tasks. I'd post a few updates on social media, and that would be it. In the past, I would spend the rest of the day developing plans, exploring opportunities, travelling, or pitching new ideas. I'd often spend large portions of my day in states of excitement, fueled by adrenaline. Of course, those days had become distant memories in recent times. It was a conscious decision of sorts, but I started exploring new activities to fill my time and prevent overthinking and worrying.

One day, Lauren and I decided to venture into the countryside. We hiked for several miles and ended up on top of a large hill overlooking the River Tees and the rolling mountains that stretched for miles around us. We stood there for about thirty minutes, holding hands, cuddling, and simply breathing, and talking. I distinctly recall feeling profoundly happy at that moment. Then, I thought about the cost of that happiness – it was free. It cost nothing beyond the fuel in our car to get there. It was a powerful realisation. I could be a billionaire or a pauper, arrive there in a Porsche or my humble Volkswagen Caddy van, and be happy or sad. Those awe-inspiring views existed at all times, and money made no difference to my ability to enjoy that moment. Regardless of what I might achieve or fail to achieve in the future, those free views and the joy of that moment will always exist. The Official Receiver couldn't take that away from us.

The moment was humbling, and it has stayed with me. It's a thought I've tried to instil in my mindset as much as possible throughout this journey. This is what people mean when they say you should enjoy changing your children's nappies and reading them a bedtime story. It suddenly made sense.

A few days later, I received a message from an elderly lady, Elizabeth, who lives near us. She told me that her husband, Alan, whom she'd been married to for over half a century, had gone into a nursing home. She wondered if I would be interested in his greenhouse. My initial reaction was one of confusion. I knew nothing about gardening, and in truth, I didn't even know what a greenhouse was for. Suddenly, I heard the choirboy in me again. I said yes, and it turned out to be one of the best, albeit unintentional, decisions I made during this difficult period.

I collected the greenhouse and brought it home. After I finished with my emails, I found myself watching YouTube videos about what you can grow in greenhouses. I don't know if I was entirely interested, or if I was just enjoying the distraction. What I did know was that most books and podcasts about mental health often talked about the countryside, exercise, and gardening as fantastic forms of self-help. So, for that reason alone, I was interested in exploring the hobby a little more. If it could make me feel better, I was willing to give it a try.

By the time summer arrived, I had read several books and magazines and found myself religiously tuning in to 'Gardeners World' on the BBC most weeks. It got me. I built several raised beds in the garden from old pallet wood and planted potatoes. There were beetroot, carrots, and tomatoes in the greenhouse, as well as strawberries for the girls. I even built an archway with the intention of growing peas as a healthy snack while I watered the garden, and I managed to get the girls involved. As time went on, Lauren also became interested, particularly once the vegetables were ready for harvesting. Being in the garden was a distraction, but it became my sanctuary over time. It was a place where I didn't need to think about anything else except the tiny seedling emerging from the soil as if it were the gearstick of the Porsche I'd once yearned for. The garden was a safe place. Or, was it?

However, it wasn't entirely without its costs, this newfound love for gardening. At times, I overthought the joy I felt in the garden and confused it with that feeling of being a fraud. I felt like I was using the garden as an excuse to avoid working hard or taking responsibility for the mess I dealt with daily alongside the Insolvency Service. Lauren would often tell me to stop being so hard on myself and to just enjoy it for what it was. But I'd often come in from the garden and just retreat to bed or slump onto the sofa. The weight of the turmoil was still there, and I felt like my new hobby was nothing more than a distraction now that I didn't have to think about growing my business. In truth, I didn't really know how I was feeling. I just didn't feel like I had many other options besides taking the girls to school, replying to some emails, and then tending to the garden. So, what else could I do?

Aside from gardening, I joined an organisation called Man v Fat Football. I stumbled upon it through a sponsored advert on Facebook. I had tried joining a gym in early 2022 but quickly realised that I absolutely hated going to the gym. And yet, I also hated being overweight and carrying what can only be described as a beer belly. I had to do something. The organisation was targeted toward people like me—middle-aged guys who wanted to play football but were perhaps past their prime in terms of peak performance. I thought it sounded perfect. On a Monday evening, I joined around 60 other members, and we played 30 minutes of football with the goal of losing weight while competing in a professionally run competition. What did I have to lose, other than weight, of course?

My friends, Chris and Mary, who had helped me through that difficult night at New Year, sent me a book, *The Alchemist* by Paulo Coelho. I haven't got the attention span or discipline required to read a large book - so in admitting that, I feel obliged to thank anyone who has come this far through my story. I know that's completely untrue, but if anything, that explains what I mean about lacking the discipline to be able to read. I can get sucked into an audiobook while driving, but that's about as much reading as I do. I was grateful for the gesture of the book, but I wasn't convinced I would read it. I was sceptical of any book being able to help the situation, to be honest. That was until I picked it up while sitting in the greenhouse one day, where I read the first chapter, and then the second, and then the third...

I completed the book in around three days. I have since read it twice more. I won't spoil the story, but it was enlightening, and it changed my scepticism almost overnight. I'd recommend it to anyone.

Chris also introduced me to a famous poem by Jalaluddin Rumi translated to English by Coleman Barks in 1997, called 'The Guest House.' It reads:

This being human is a guest house.
Every morning a new arrival.

A joy, a depression, a meanness,
some momentary awareness comes
as an unexpected visitor.

Welcome and entertain them all!

Even if they're a crowd of sorrows,
who violently sweep your house
empty of its furniture,
still, treat each guest honourably.
He may be clearing you out
for some new delight.

The dark thought, the shame, the malice,
meet them at the door laughing,
and invite them in.

Be grateful for whoever comes,
because each has been sent
as a guide from beyond.

Copyright 1997 Coleman Barks.
Shared with permission.

It's short, and it was written in the 13th century, over 800 years ago. Rumi got it, even then. Anxiety, depression, stress, mental health. It's not a new thing. It's been around as long as mankind, and Rumi captured it in his poem centuries ago. That helped me with some perspective. More importantly, his works helped me to process how to handle what I was going through. The crowd of swallows could well be the Official Receiver. It could be the voice in my own head, torturing my soul and beating up any ounce of dignity that I had left.

Welcome! Entertain the voices. Be excited for what opportunities and mysteries might lay ahead in your life as these old, painful scars heal. Be grateful for those scars.

I ordered a print of the poem and taped it to the wall outside my bedroom. I wanted to use it as a reminder every morning when I woke up and took the journey across my landing in preparation for a new day of difficult conversations and fragile emotions. No matter what things were flowing through my mind each morning, I wanted to try my best to acknowledge them.

Distraction was, for me, the best remedy. So long as I could keep busy with things and keep those twenty sales coming in, I could remain calm and embrace what I was selling to myself as a new way of life. A much slower pace, filled with the green grasses of the garden and the bounty of homegrown vegetables. I could work as and when I needed to - and in truth, not be pinned down to the business as I had been in previous years. I could take my time. The Porsche no longer mattered. What mattered was keeping the roof over my girls' heads and enjoying Hand Dyed Shoe Co. for what it was - a micro-business that earned me a living.

'Keep it simple, make the sales you need, and enjoy your time with the kids,' Bill told me.

Chapter 22

Home

The Official Receiver had declared interest in only a few assets that I owned; my van, my life insurance policy, and the equity in our home.

With the van, they gave me a choice. They would repossess it and give me £1,350 in order to buy a replacement vehicle to ensure I could get to work. My van wasn't worth a great deal. I'd had a small accident the year before, which meant it was partially damaged. My insurance company wrote it off, and I was able to buy it back from them rather than scrap it. I had it fixed up with my payout, but it still had a few scars. They said that if I could find £1,000, I could pay the Insolvency Service that sum, and in return, I could keep my van. I preferred to keep my van because, to replace it, I wasn't convinced I'd get something more reliable for the £1,350 they were willing to give me to replace it with. So, we secured the vehicle by paying the Insolvency Service £1,000.

My camera was a few years old. When I bought it in 2017, I paid about £2,500 for it alongside the lenses. Peter, who had guided me through my application when filing for bankruptcy, said I didn't need to declare it, but I was anxious about not declaring anything that they might be interested in. For me, I felt like I'd rather just tell them I had this thing now than have any sort of repercussions later. So, I declared it. Luckily for me, once they researched a Canon 6D's resale value, they came back to me and told me that they had no interest in my camera.

Life insurance came out of the blue somewhat. Peter had never mentioned that they might have an interest in that, which in hindsight makes perfect sense. After all, if I died tomorrow, and my policy paid out, my creditors needed to be paid before my wife and children. It was nominal, but the Official Receiver offered me a deal of £100 in order to keep my insurance policies in place with my wife and children as the beneficiaries. It was a no-brainer. We paid the £100 from our wages at our next payday.

It took a few months into bankruptcy before my biggest asset was brought to the table: my half of the equity in our home. It's not an easy thing to place a valuation on because there are, of course, many variables that come into play when valuing property, a major one being timing. At the time that the Official Receiver began the conversation around our house, the property market was experiencing a surge in pricing. We were so nervous about what the property might be valued because, unlike when you want to sell your house, if you don't want to sell your house and, in fact, you want to keep it with as little damage done to your immediate finances, then you don't want it to be valued too high. We knew the most likely outcome of this process was going to be that the service would put a charge on the property. So, whatever figure they concluded was the value of my equity, they would force the charge, and when our next mortgage renewal was due, we would have to add that figure to the borrowing in order to pay off the service's charge. It wasn't a pleasant thought, but if the charge was affordable, then it was probably going to be the best outcome and realistically, our only option.

We went back and forth a few times disputing the valuation of my equity. In order to give ourselves some understanding and evidence, we had three estate agents come out to value our home. The valuations came out between £310,000 and £320,000 respectively. We sent the valuations into the service, alongside a compelling argument as to why we felt the house was worth no more than £315,000. It was a gut-wrenching wait. There could well have been a counterclaim that it was, in fact, worth more than what we were suggesting, and it may well have sold for more on the normal, open market, but given that the Insolvency Service would be looking for a quick sale should they wish to force it through, they would have to find us alternative accommodation because of the children, plus the significant blockage in the process that was my wife, Lauren, who wasn't bankrupt or implicated in any of my contractual credit agreements. It was agreed at £315,000.

What this meant was that once the balance of the mortgage was taken off the property value, and the combined equity was halved, my half was worth £27,000.

We agreed on the valuation. We assumed that they would then start the process of applying a charge to the property for that amount and that when we were ready to remortgage, we would have to add the figure to the loan. Before we got there, though, we wanted to see if the third option of agreeing to a deal now for us to buy back the financial interest in the property was one we could explore. So, we made an offer: £3,500. We knew it was derisory, but that was everything we had in the bank on that day. If, by some miracle, it was acceptable, we would pay them that figure today, and we knew that from that point forward, our home would be safe.

I was refreshing my email every 15 seconds after I'd sent it. Nothing was coming back. So, we waited. And we waited. Four days later, we received the reply.

> *Dear Simon,*
>
> *The Official Receiver is unable to accept the offer of £3,500.*
>
> *With regards to placing the charge on property, as per insolvency policy, we will be offering the*

> *case to an Insolvency Practitioner as the equity is above £25,000.*
>
> *Kind Regards,*
>
> *Official Receiver*

It was a blow. What we took from it was that no cash below £25,000 would be acceptable. What made things worse was the threat that they were about to pass the case to an Insolvency Practitioner - which basically meant they were going to pass it outside of the Insolvency Service to deal with my case. I was desperately disappointed. I was praying that the offer of £3,500, although unlikely, would have been enough for the service to accept, given that I simply didn't have anything else. But, they knew that a charge of up to £27,000, although more costly for them to secure, would ultimately see the service recoup a much larger sum from my estate.

I really didn't want them to pass the case on because we felt that this came with all kinds of potential further consequences. *What if the Insolvency Practitioner appointed disagreed with the valuation of our home and wanted to open that can of worms?* My anxiety and stress levels were overwhelming.

Lauren and I decided that we should go back to the Official Receiver and make another offer. We needed to know what figure would be acceptable so that we knew what we were dealing with. We called the Official Receiver and asked what they would accept. They refused to give us a number and just told us to make an offer, so we did. We offered £4,500. It was entirely hypothetical because we didn't have the money. A few more days passed before we received the rejection. We went back with £5,500, then £6,500. We offered £9,000, then £10,000, then £12,000. We told them each time that these offers were meaningless because we didn't have the money waiting to be transferred, but they refused to tell us what the 'acceptable amount' would be, reminding us that it would need to be closer to the valuation of £27,000. It felt like a game of cat and mouse. We were desperate, and they probably knew it. Peter told us to string it out as long as we could, but we needed closure. We got to £18,000 when the Official Receiver changed their response. They said if we could pay £20,000, they would accept.

It was quite possibly the worst display of negotiation in the history of business deals, but this wasn't business. If it was poker, I might as well have been playing with transparent cards, and they knew it. But this was our lives and our children's lives. They knew we were desperate, and they knew we would keep returning with another offer. They knew we were offering invisible money after £3,500, so there was little motivation to say yes to £4,500 - they might as well push it as high as we were willing to gamble our invisible cash.

It was a sickening feeling. We didn't have £20,000. We were both from working-class backgrounds, and our families didn't have £20,000, we knew that. We didn't have a rich uncle or a friend of the family we could turn to for that kind of money. We had £3,500, and there was no way we could find another £16,500 in such a short space of time.

I was lying in bed when it came to me. Lauren had already fallen asleep, the TV was still on, and I was lying there, scrolling on my phone. The house was silent - it was about midnight. I was worrying about what was going to happen, but I wasn't actively seeking a solution. I have no recollection of where the idea came from; it wasn't a conscious decision. But, something in that moment, in that silent house, triggered something in my brain, and I felt a sudden swoosh of raging butterflies in the pit of my stomach. A solution? Perhaps!

I didn't have £16,500. But, what I did have at my mercy was a brand. If I could create something to sell, a special product, limited edition, and I could sell enough of them, the profits we made from that product might well get us a lot closer. I sat bolt upright with my back against my pillow. I grabbed my laptop, and I began designing a special edition shoe - a sneaker. All of a sudden, I was running, and for the first time in a very long time, I had those feelings again. I created the design, a classic sneaker style that was largely made up of a hand-drawn textile pattern I had created a few years back. On the back of the sneakers, I wrote the words 'Thank You' on a small cut of leather. These were special edition Simon Bourne sneakers. That was the easy part, I thought.

The next thing I had to do was much tougher. I had to tell the world what I was doing. I have never set out to sell anything without authenticity, but the authenticity behind this particular product was raw, embarrassing and humiliating. Putting that out there in the big wide world was a terrifying thought. We hadn't told anyone about the bankruptcy beyond close family members and a couple of friends. There was a clear feeling of discomfort amongst certain members of the family when the depths of my financial problems became apparent. In putting it out there in the public eye, everybody knows. The world knows. The Insolvency Service could know. Friends of friends. All of those people who see me as some kind of entrepreneurial wizard would know I was a failure. My old colleagues, who had all thought I was going to go on to great things when I left the public sector. The 20,000 people who I didn't know but were following me on LinkedIn. They would know. *And what would the consequences be? Perhaps they'd not trust my brand anymore. Maybe they'd think I was a fraud.* It was only 12 hours before this moment that I was posting about a fantastic customer experience that we were celebrating - and now I was back online posting about the fact the business was in fact a new business because I was bankrupt. I feared those more immediate family members who didn't know the situation seeing it. My siblings, cousins, aunts and uncles. This might come as a bit of a shock to them. They might be angry that I was bringing the family name into disrepute. They might be pissed off that I didn't tell them first.

I asked myself one question in a variety of ways: *Would I care if people thought I was a failure if I pulled this off? Would I sell my personal embarrassment and shame to be able to tell Lauren I'd fixed it?* Would it matter if my family thought I was an idiot if I didn't have to move my kids out of the home they loved? The truth is, I didn't think about any of the shame as I sat there. I didn't give much thought to what anybody else would think about my decision to share the news I was bankrupt publicly, other than Lauren - and I knew she would be more overjoyed with solving the £16k problem than she would be worried about the court of public opinion. Why would I? I was running, and I had stars in my eyes. I don't think a great deal at all when I'm running, I just run - get one foot in front of the other. I was fantasising about how Lauren would wake up in the morning, and I'd be able to tell her I'd solved the problem. My eyes were glazed over, and I was fully focused, albeit taking many long breaths in and out.

I carefully crafted my post.

This is probably the most personal and sickeningly difficult post I've ever written.

Earlier this year I was declared bankrupt as a result of COVID (amongst other things). It has, without a doubt, been the toughest year of my life and there have been some pretty dark moments, to say the least. I'm exceptionally proud of how far I have come.

Yesterday, I received the news from the Insolvency Service that in order to bring a close to my bankruptcy and remove the threat that my home could be repossessed, I needed to find £20,000.

Truthfully, I don't have it. But, the one thing I do have is this beautiful, beautiful brand and so in order to try and raise the funds that my family and I need, I've come up with a special, one-off, unique sneaker design featuring my hand-drawn, Liberty-inspired artwork.

I am going to make and sell only 99 pairs of these, and after that, I am never ever going to make them again. The 100th pair will not be sold, but it will sit on a shelf in my home as a piece of history, a memory, and a reminder of how great people and humanity really are.

So, if you love the brand, enjoy my posts, and

> *would like to be part of saving my home, ending what has been the most difficult time for my family and me, we wholeheartedly thank you.*
>
> *It goes without saying, that was not an easy post to write, but well, my hope is that it just might well be the most valuable post I've ever written.*
>
> *You can order yours here:*
>
> *handdyedshoeco.com/limitededitionsneaker*

I carefully calculated that the profits from the 99 pairs, after all taxes and duties, would yield nearly £6,500 as a lump sum. If we added that to our initial £3,500, we'd have £10k, and we would be halfway there. Perhaps we could then approach family members to help us raise the other half.

Within 2 minutes of hitting the post button, the first order came in – Julia Hewett. Shortly after, we received orders from Richard Gallant, Darren Stones, Stephen Davis, Roy Darby, and Richard Bacon... My heart pounded like a rock and roll drummer in my chest. How could I sleep? I lay there, responding to messages from well-wishers, many of them complete strangers who had seen the post and wanted to wish me luck. Some offered to send me money or suggested I set up a Just Giving campaign so they could donate small amounts. I declined their offers. While I was grateful for the gesture, I didn't want to be a sob story. I was comfortable selling a product and giving something beautiful in return for donations, but I didn't want anything for free. Charities needed donations for far more important reasons than I did, but these gestures were humbling and inspiring.

One of my American customers, Dan O'Neal, contacted me and expressed his admiration for how open I was. He shared his own daunting personal journey, which was, in some aspects, more challenging than mine. Dan was, by my estimation, a very wealthy man. His initial shoe order with me totalled around £6,000 for about a dozen pairs – a record single order at the time. He asked how much I needed, indicating his willingness to help. Once again, I declined his offer and encouraged him to order more sneakers, as that would be the best way he could assist me.

I started receiving messages from other people who had been bankrupt, praising my openness. It was an unexpected turn of events. I had just shared my story, and now I was receiving messages of adoration. Many of these people had kept their financial struggles secret for decades until reading my post. I felt powerful and influential. People commended my bravery, although I didn't see it as brave; I considered it desperate and necessary. Others shared their battles with depression, anxiety, divorce, gambling, and death. All of these were life scars of trauma in their own right.

I didn't remember what time I fell asleep, or if I even slept. I likely passed out with my phone firmly in my hand, the blue tones of LinkedIn lighting up my face.

Morning came with the usual madness of getting the girls ready for school. I was constantly following Lauren around the house, trying to find a private moment to share what I had done. We had managed to sell 19 pairs of the limited edition sneakers. In the end, I didn't need to tell her; she saw the post on Facebook. She didn't say anything, but I could see the concern in her face. Lauren wasn't one to share my passion for running; she cared more about public perception. Her immediate thoughts revolved around what people, especially our family, would say. She wasn't angry with me, but I sensed her wish that I had spoken to her about it first. I understood her perspective, but I also knew that had I consulted her, she would have likely been resistant due to concerns about public perception. Despite her reservations, she supported me and expressed her pride in my decision to share my story, even if it wasn't the way she would have done things. We both knew that we were right in our own ways, and most importantly, she understood that this was my way of dealing with our challenges on our long and arduous journey.

Naturally, we received phone calls and messages the following day from concerned family members and friends. Bankruptcy wasn't a topic discussed publicly, and public shaming was a part of the threat that came with it. People asked if our names would appear in the newspaper, expressed concerns about our children, and feared bailiffs and debt collectors coming to our door. It wasn't pleasant, but I attributed most of it to a lack of understanding of the process. Thanks to Neville and Peter, I had a better understanding of the process and did my best to reassure them. I also explained my plan to raise the necessary funds to secure our home. It was uncomfortable and brought shame to our loved ones, compounding the shame I had already brought upon myself. However, Lauren was a pillar of support, reminding me of her pride and understanding each time we had a private moment. That was all I needed.

As the days passed, orders for the sneakers kept coming in, and we neared our target. Bill supported the plan, recognising that once this issue was resolved, I would be in a much better mental state to move forward with the business. We reluctantly approached family members to see if anyone could help us raise the remaining £10,000. It wasn't easy. As I mentioned earlier, we were a typical working-class family, and that kind of money wasn't just sitting in a savings account. One person even offered to cancel their holiday to help us, while another said they could scrape together a couple of thousand pounds. It was a grim and guilt-inducing task, but we had limited options.

Then Bill had an idea. During dinner one evening, he joined us at the table, and after discussing the usual business matters, he raised a suggestion I hadn't considered. 'What if we injected some money into the business, sold some equity to an investor, and you could receive it as a bonus on your salary?' he proposed. 'Do you know anyone interested in investing in the brand?'

I did. I couldn't believe what I was hearing. This was Bill's business and equity, not mine. He had already played a significant role in rescuing the business and providing me with a job. Over the years, many people have expressed interest in investing. In the days immediately following my limited edition sneaker campaign, I received several messages from individuals interested in buying the business and taking it forward. I had largely ignored these opportunities, as Bill had already handled that aspect. Furthermore, many had expressed interest in being part of the story before Hand Dyed Shoe Co. Ltd. went bankrupt, but they were discouraged by the significant debt. Now that the debt is gone, they might be more interested in a new business without such financial burdens. Perhaps they could see the potential.

The next day, I reached out to a few individuals to discuss selling a portion of the equity in FCC Retail Trading Ltd. By the time I sat down for dinner that evening, I had three offers to present to Bill. Each offer entailed a £40,000 investment in exchange for a 20% stake in FCC Retail Trading Ltd. The investors understood that the first £20,000 of that money would go directly to the Insolvency Service to secure my family home. The remaining £20,000 would be used to stabilise the business and provide it with some breathing room for the next few months as things settled down.

I immediately thought of Dan O'Neal, the American customer who was a fan of the business and me. He had praised the shoes he received and the overall experience. His initial order for about a dozen pairs totalled around £6,000, setting a record for a single order at the time. I was curious about his success and spent a few days conducting due diligence. Everything I found indicated that he was a genuine and successful individual. His motivation was primarily to help. I had learned from my experience with Neville to trust people unless they gave me a reason not to, and Dan had been straightforward from the moment we spoke. He had no prior knowledge of the opportunity to buy equity when he ordered his shoes, so there seemed to be little risk in the deal. Like me, he was a family man, and he had achieved considerable success in business. It was a compelling proposition. We documented everything via email, and the agreement was reached quickly. Dan purchased a 20% stake in FCC Retail Trading Ltd for £40,000.

There was no celebration. I still felt the pressure of the situation and was anxious. As I write this chapter in hindsight, I find it hard to believe the extraordinary sequence of events that unfolded, but that's exactly what happened. This deal saved our home.

Within a few days, we sent the £20,000 to the Insolvency Service and received legal documentation confirming that they were no longer interested in any other assets within my estate. The sales from the sneakers helped support the business and relieved the immediate pressure to sell, although I still grappled with the aftermath of this incredible journey. We were able to visit the family members who had generously offered to help us raise much-needed funds, thanking them with flowers and a card. It was wonderful to tell them that we no longer required the money and that they could proceed with their plans. It felt like a miracle, a gift, perhaps a reward for our openness and for sharing my story publicly. It was a blessing, especially considering the hours of phone calls and messages exchanged with strangers who reached out to me when I shared my bankruptcy experience.

It was over. I could breathe. We could breathe.

Chapter 23

Mental Wealth

Over the following few weeks, I felt like I was living in a daze. I had stopped taking my antidepressant tablets; they didn't seem to be making a difference, and to be honest, I often forgot to take them. I continued to spend a lot of time in the garden, tending to vegetables, crafting, and simply passing the days. The business was barely holding on – and when I say that, I mean it was barely surviving. There was a new crisis in the air, a cost-of-living crisis. Economic inflation was soaring, with energy costs now three times what they were before the COVID-19 pandemic. Food prices had doubled, and fuel was around 50% more expensive. People were anxious; even the UK's wealthier citizens weren't spending like they were in 2019, and that was clear. Consequently, over several months, we were struggling to produce even the 20 pairs I needed to secure my salary. It left me feeling uneasy because the last thing I wanted was to end up in the same dire situation and be forced to make difficult decisions again. I was trapped in a cycle of torment in my mind. When I was in the garden, I felt like I wasn't trying hard enough to generate sales. Yet, when I was in the studio, I often found myself staring at a computer screen with few ideas about how to improve the situation. I was consciously trying to stay calm because having come this far through the crisis, I was determined to avoid starting another one.

Dan was now a part of the team. Both he and Bill were the official owners, and I was essentially responsible for running the brand, with the exception of anything related to bank accounts, finances, or signatures. I was putting in considerable effort to establish connections and foster a transparent business environment where everyone had a clear understanding of our sales projections. I hoped that if Bill could gain a better grasp of this aspect, we could more effectively predict our cash flow and manage the financial side of the business. Dan, on the other hand, was observing from a distance and would provide his expertise and guidance as necessary or whenever he saw fit. Everything was in place, ready to transform into a more profitable venture, but we were grappling with the challenge of generating the necessary sales to keep things afloat.

Dan's £20,000 investment had been instrumental in clearing some of the historical debts that we had carried over into the new business, leaving us with roughly £10,000 in reserves. However, as the months passed and we approached Christmas in 2022, that £10,000 was slowly dwindling. I could feel myself reaching those familiar stress levels as the funds started to disappear. My enthusiasm was waning, and my motivation was fading. The once energetic stride had turned into a sluggish dawdle. It became clear that it was time to walk away; I couldn't continue any longer. FCC Retail Trading Ltd. seemed to be following the same path as Hand Dyed Shoe Co. Ltd., and I found myself torn between the tales of entrepreneurial tenacity and the necessity of recognising when it was time to let go. I didn't want to give up, not even in the slightest, but if we couldn't make this work financially, at least to cover my salary, then we had no choice but to stop, and I needed to explore alternative means of making a living.

As we entered 2023, I could feel my mental health crumbling and it wasn't long before the thoughts of suicide returned. I tried my best to keep the depths of those thoughts largely to myself; I didn't want to burden Lauren with my inner struggles. But, she could see through my facade. I had lost my enjoyment for the garden, and even going to work had become a joyless endeavour. Nothing brought me joy anymore. How could it? I vividly recall browsing job websites and feeling even more disheartened. Every job listing I came across held no appeal; I couldn't envision myself doing those roles or caring about them, and at times, I felt inadequate for them. It was a futile exercise that only added to my sense of despair. I was adrift, lost in a sea of uncertainty.

My daily routine had become a monotonous cycle. It

typically began with the school run in the morning, followed by aimless visits to coffee shops, where I'd sit in a fog of uncertainty. My hours in the garden felt empty, devoid of the joy they once brought. I'd occasionally muster the energy to send a few emails and make updates to my website, but my efforts were lacklustre at best. Social media became a pit of procrastination that I'd fall into, and I'd mindlessly engage in phone games, even though I derived no pleasure from them. I was trapped in a waiting game, desperately hoping that tomorrow might hold something different, something brighter.

But beneath it all, I carried a heavy burden of guilt for feeling this way. *How dare I feel like this after coming through all the things I'd come through? How ungrateful am I to still be thinking about suicide having come this far? How disrespectful is this to Bill, Dan, Neville and Peter?* The overthinking was unbearable.

In early March, I took a walk around Durham City, and as I strolled along the riverbanks, I couldn't help but notice every bench I passed. Each one bore a plaque with a name, usually in memory of someone. But to my surprise, every single bench seemed to bear my name, Simon. It felt as though a haunting message was etched into every one of them, a message meant for me.

Around that time, there was a news story that had captured my attention, involving a young lady who had gone missing near a river. I became almost obsessed with the details of her case, constantly refreshing news websites and delving into research about her. It was a profoundly tragic situation, and yet, I found myself fixated on it. I kept thinking. *Tragic, indeed. Would my death be perceived as tragic?* When news broke that they had found her, it hit me like a ton of bricks. I read the media reports as though they were about me. In my mind, I was the one in that river. I was dead. I read the interviews, and the statements, imagining them being spoken by Lauren about me.

These thoughts led me to contemplate my life insurance. I found myself considering how to make my death look like an accident so Lauren would receive some form of payout. I was in trouble.

One morning, I called Bill and sharply snapped at him when he commented on our lack of sales. I even video-called Dan, who was in Romania with his wife at the time and broke down in tears. I confessed to him that I believed the business was doomed to fail again, and I apologised profusely for what I saw as a colossal waste of his time, money, and energy. I felt responsible for the dismal performance as if I had sold them both a broken dream. *Who did I think I was, after all?*

Lauren was understandably concerned about me. I had

broken down in tears on a couple of occasions, and she could see that I was spiralling. After our emotional conversations, she often reminded me not to be so hard on myself, and she was absolutely right. I was my own harshest critic. Despite all the progress I had made in terms of my circumstances, I still felt deeply insecure. Inside, I believed I was ugly and a failure. I saw myself as an idiot, naive, and foolish. It was as if I had become those negative labels.

I realised that I needed to take action; this couldn't continue. I had been avoiding seeing a doctor because I knew they would likely recommend going back on the antidepressant tablets. But I had to do something. So, I made an appointment.

A few days before the appointment, my sister Rachel came to visit. She was genuinely worried about me. Rachel and I have a unique bond; we can go months without speaking, yet she's my best friend, and she always seems to understand me. We were in the car when she started asking me probing questions about how I was feeling. At first, I resisted opening up. I didn't want therapy; I couldn't be bothered. But Rachel, as she often did, managed to strike the right chord. She asked me, 'Why do you think you're a failure?' I didn't have a clear answer; I just felt like I was one because of all the mistakes I had made. She then posed another question, 'Is that what you truly believe people think of you?' It was a thought-provoking question, and I couldn't answer it.

Rachel went on to remind me of the support I had given her during challenging times in her life. She listed my accomplishments, saying, 'You had the courage to start a company. You've been a journalist, a photographer, a website designer, a shoe entrepreneur. You faced bankruptcy, sold your brand, and you're still here, relentlessly pursuing success. Do you realise how many people would have given up by now? How many would never have even started what you did?' Her words were comforting, but I responded with, 'Well, that's what you're supposed to say; you're my sister.' Rachel didn't let me dismiss her words so easily; she firmly stated, 'That's what people see in you: strength, resilience, determination, ambition, love, and kindness.'

'THAT'S WHAT PEOPLE SEE!'

Rachel's next remarks hit me harder than anything I'd heard before. She expressed her concern about my marriage, and I felt as if my stomach had plummeted down to my toes. Suddenly, there was an immense weight on my shoulders, pushing me deeper into the car seat. I held my breath, trying desperately not to react, but I needed to hear what she had to say. *What had Lauren confided in her?* It was the first time I had ever worried about my marriage.

As far as I could tell, Lauren and I had a perfect relationship. We were a team, and we had each other's backs, no matter what. She was the reason I was still fighting, and I cared about her and our children more than anything else in the world. My love for them far outweighed any concerns about myself. The idea that maybe Lauren's feelings weren't as strong as mine was a crushing blow, worse than any financial hardship or bankruptcy. I would happily lose my home if it meant I could keep her. My mental health was already fragile, but the thought of losing my wife and children was unbearable. They were my mental wealth, the most valuable part of my life. Until that moment, I had never truly worried that they might leave me.

'She's tired, Simon,' Rachel said. 'She's exhausted. She's doing all the housework. She's going to work, doing 13-hour shifts in a hospital. She's organising the girls. She's worried every single second of every single day about you.' Rachel's words swirled around my head like a tornado. It was a force of truth. It was undeniable. I wasn't doing anything at home to share the load. I was tired too, but I just couldn't find the motivation. Instead, I'd leave things undone, and Lauren would inevitably take care of them. I had been trying to shield Lauren from the full extent of my thoughts, but she knew, and she carried that worry with her every time she left me alone. She went to work concerned that she might return to find me dead. It was a perspective I hadn't considered before, and I knew, now more than ever, that I couldn't lose her.

Unable to keep my thoughts to myself for long, I talked to Lauren about it. I asked her directly if she was waiting for me to get better, planning to leave me and take the girls once she felt I could manage on my own. Her eyes welled with tears. She assured me that it had never crossed her mind, and Rachel had misunderstood a conversation about housework. She told me she loved me and that we were a team, a family. She wouldn't change anything about me or our relationship. I was sceptical, uncertain about what to believe. What if she was just saying this to encourage me to get better? I realised I needed to see a doctor immediately.

I managed to secure an appointment for the following day. As I expected, my GP was stern when I confessed that I had stopped taking my medication. She pointed out that this was likely the reason my thoughts and feelings had become so extreme. When I shared my fear that Lauren might leave me once I got better, she inquired if I had discussed it with her, which I had. She emphasised the importance of consistently taking my medication and suggested I see her every week until she was confident enough to discharge me. I promised her that I would take the medication seriously, and I meant it. I had to do everything in my power to end these episodes. I couldn't continue tormenting myself with thoughts of suicide – not only for my sake but for my family's as well. They were suffering because of me, and that realisation was enough to make me take my medication seriously. Beyond that, I began exploring other strategies to help me through difficult times. I started listening to podcasts, researching therapy options, and investing in self-help books.

I also committed to writing the journals that had been recommended to me months earlier.

Chapter 24

Soled Out!

Journaling wasn't a natural habit for me. While I enjoyed creative writing and saw language as a form of art, I didn't routinely document my life in a diary. My grandad used to advise me to read the dictionary, a peculiar suggestion I didn't grasp back then, but I now understood the importance of expanding my vocabulary and using language artistically. Instead of reading the dictionary, I relished discovering new words and expressing myself through language. However, when I started journaling, it wasn't an immediate transition. It took several weeks, perhaps even months after I visited the GP before I began writing. I struggled to figure out what to write about.

Things began to change after I publicly announced my bankruptcy on social media. In June 2022, I recorded a podcast with an entrepreneur named Ashleigh King, where we discussed the challenges of running small businesses and our personal journeys. During that off-air conversation, I mentioned my ambition to write a book someday, a goal Ashleigh shared. My intention transformed from 'I'd love to write a book,' to 'I am going to write a book.' The prospect of achieving this goal reignited my motivation, and we set a date for our first writing session. By that time, I had also become invested in the idea of journaling as a form of therapy.

When I began journaling, it was in a digital document, not the traditional pen-and-paper method recommended by my doctor. I gravitated towards the digital format because of my comfort with technology. On the day I started writing, I found myself immediately immersed in the events of 23rd December 2021. This was the moment I felt compelled to explore in depth. I wanted to understand the profound emotions I had experienced and help others comprehend them as well. While I am usually good at discussing my feelings and emotions, particularly with Lauren, I sometimes struggle to articulate the depth of my emotions concisely and accurately. My thoughts can jump between topics, from overthinking to anxiety, stress, or depression, ultimately leading to a simplified conclusion that I'm just a complete mess. This can be frustrating, so writing provides me with a more accurate way to convey my feelings.

I am also prone to taking responsibility to an extreme degree. I hold strong beliefs and values, and I am passionate about discussing topics I care about, even when they are challenging. If a friend is making poor choices or behaving selfishly, I would make an effort to have a conversation with them to help them recognise the impact of their actions. However, if they react negatively or others suggest I shouldn't have intervened, my immediate conclusion is that I am a nasty person. I tend to withdraw or assume I must be wrong if someone offers a different perspective. This can lead to feelings of cruelty or unkindness and make me question the authenticity of my good intentions. My inclination to concede in the face of adversity can frustrate Lauren. In disagreements, I become even more passionate about my opinions with her, which can create tension. As my passion intensifies, Lauren finds it challenging to engage in conversation with me. My most infamous saying, 'I must be a twat then,' often emerges, followed by Lauren's response of 'I never said that.' She's correct; she didn't say that. However, I'm vocalising where my self-esteem stands at that moment. If someone disagrees with me, my automatic assumption is that I must be wrong, triggering insecurity. I constantly evaluate and analyse my character, attempting to determine if I am good or bad, kind or greedy.

Writing my book, Soled Out!, was a journey that started with the most challenging day of my life. Starting with that day provided a sense of closure, an understanding of my own experience, and ownership of my story. I take responsibility for it. It felt like a way to help others understand what I went through, but most importantly, for myself to understand it.

The structure of the book unfolded naturally. I didn't

plan it meticulously; I wrote it honestly and authentically, letting the story flow as it needed to. In the early days of writing, I felt a surge of adrenaline that kept me up into the early hours as I poured my thoughts onto the page. However, when I reached chapter 6, the story of Colin Elrick and the real beginning of the business, I felt my momentum stall. I couldn't find the words. My mind felt cold, and the excitement turned into a whirlwind of complex emotions.

Writer's block is a common obstacle for authors, and I was no exception. The success stories, like Colin's order - the first ever order I took for a pair of shoes - was tainted with arrogance and ugliness in my mind because of what followed. It was difficult to write about them without feeling like a fraud. This roadblock lasted for almost four months, but I refused to quit. I saw the rewards of completing this book as greater than any award or accolade. I was determined not to be a quitter and find another way, just as I had with challenges in the past.

My introduction to Eleanor Baggaley, who helped me with the book, came through Ann English, the lady who had worked with me on my Visual Map in 2017. Eleanor offered her professional services to help me overcome writer's block and take me through the publishing process. We reached an agreement based on future book sales since I couldn't afford her upfront. I was grateful for this arrangement as it gave me renewed energy and allowed me to focus on finishing my story.

I intentionally wrote this entire book by myself, without sharing it with anyone, even my wife, until it was published. I wanted the narrative to be entirely mine, free from external influences or doubts about its truthfulness. This book is my story, and in holding it, I feel a sense of closure on the events that transpired. It's an achievement that tops all others, and I'm grateful to anyone reading it.

Writing a book that flips the narrative of a failed entrepreneur who faced bankruptcy, contemplated suicide, and lived with regret and disappointment has been my greatest achievement. It has given me closure, resilience, determination, and a stronger foundation for the future. When you write your story down, you realise how far you've come and the hurdles you've overcome. You feel proud and you realise that you're not as bad as you perhaps think you are. Those hurdles are there for a reason, and today, I am not 'Soled Out!' I am sold on my strength, spirit, and resilience.

Chapter 25

Redemption

The day I was discharged from bankruptcy, exactly twelve months after my application, was on 26th April 2023. Lauren and I had planned to go out for a celebratory meal, however, we couldn't afford it. Still, we cherished the evening and reflected on the journey we had been through over the dining room table with a bottle of wine.

During this time, I thought a lot about the people who had supported me on this challenging journey, particularly Neville and Peter. I had visited Neville just before Christmas and gave him a pair of my limited-edition sneakers along with a nice bottle of scotch. He was appreciative, as always, and even offered to pay for them, but I declined. For Peter, who wasn't particularly into shoes or alcohol, I wanted to find a gift that would truly bring him joy. Knowing how much he enjoyed his allotment and his chickens, I decided to give him a unique gift that symbolises life itself.

I had never bought live chickens before, and I wasn't sure where to find them. After asking around at a few farms, I located a small poultry holding not far from my home. I arranged to meet Peter at his allotment, and as I arrived, he gave me a tour of his plot and introduced me to his flock. It was clear that these chickens meant the world to him. During our conversation, he opened up about his personal struggles, including going through a divorce after over three decades of marriage.

I thanked Peter for being there for me and my family during my difficult times. I explained that I couldn't repay him with money, but I wanted to show my gratitude in a meaningful way. I then presented him with a cardboard hen house and inside were two chickens named Daisy and Penny.

I told Peter, 'I couldn't think of anything greater to buy you than life, Peter. Here are two chickens to add to your flock. I hope they bring you the same happiness that my Daisy and Penny bring to me.'

We both teared up and shared a heartfelt hug. Peter was overwhelmed and said it was the greatest gift he had ever received. I felt proud and grateful for the opportunity to express my gratitude.

As we said our goodbyes at the gates of his allotment, Peter hurried up the street with his new companions, eager to introduce Daisy and Penny to one of his allotment friends. I like to think that Peter is enjoying fresh eggs every morning, and they taste just a bit more special because of the story behind Daisy and Penny.

A few weeks after being discharged, Bill informed me that he was retiring from his job and no longer wanted to be involved with FCC Retail. It was a mix of emotions for me because when he took it on, I had hoped he would do more than just maintain the business. I had wanted him to bring his experience and act as a mentor. While I had always hoped that someday I might own the business again, or at least a portion of it, it wasn't my main motivation. What mattered most to me was that it continued to exist. The name above the door wasn't important; I loved it regardless. Unfortunately, I didn't have the money to buy the business back from him, but he didn't want anything and was more than happy to hand it over. It wasn't trading as well as he had initially thought when I first sold it to him, and honestly, I don't think he believed it would ever be more than a small micro-business. I called the Insolvency Service to ask for their permission to appoint myself as a director of FCC Retail Trading Ltd. They had no objections and wished me well.

My mental health has undoubtedly improved since I started taking the Sertraline tablets correctly. I take 100mg per day, and I haven't missed a single tablet since my initial meeting with the GP. A few weeks after our first meeting, my GP told me that I didn't need to attend weekly appointments anymore and that I could simply get in touch if I felt the need. To date, I haven't experienced negative thoughts to the degree where I felt the need to contact her. I've made changes to my routine and have become much more focused both at work and in my personal life. I'm not spending as much time in the garden, but when I am there, I'm fully present. My Gardener's World subscription is still active, and I try to enjoy it when the magazine arrives.

I've taken a job as a taxi driver to supplement my income from FCC Retail Trading Ltd. If someone had told me a few months ago that I would be doing this, I would have dismissed the idea. Ironically, I'm enjoying it. I leave the house in the morning for two hours, taking a group of children with behavioural needs to school. I've become friends with a young boy who reminds me of myself when I was his age (11). He seeks attention, and I try to give it to him as much as possible. He is highly intelligent and loves chess, often telling me all about it during our trips. I ask him questions, not because I'm particularly interested in chess, but because I'm genuinely interested in him and his interests. We take turns naming countries around the world, and we're both equally excited when we come up with more unique places. Eritrea, Djibouti, and Kiribati are my personal favourites. I've spent time talking to him about manifesting his dreams and have shared bits of my story with him, including my experiences in journalism, photography, and the shoe business. I feel like I'm making a difference, and since I started, I haven't encountered any behavioural issues with him. The experience has been incredibly inspiring, and I'm convinced that he's going to have a challenging but highly successful life, even if he may not realise it himself. I'll be sad when he leaves for secondary school in a few weeks. He's helped me a lot, even if he doesn't know it.

The business is secure. It's not setting any records, but it's doing well enough. With my taxi driving job in place, the number of required sales per month has been reduced by almost half, which is manageable. I would describe my mood as calm. I've thought a lot about that word, calm.

I believe that calm is what the vast majority of us seek in life. Some may say they're seeking happiness, but true happiness is often fleeting. It's a temporary emotion that provides a surge of adrenaline, and while we all enjoy it, it's not a realistic permanent state of being. Another word people often use is contentment, but I don't aspire to that either. Contentment implies that we should accept our current circumstances and be satisfied with what we have. I can't do that.

I find happiness in various aspects of my life. I love the version of myself when I'm running, chasing after the next challenge, helping customers, developing relationships, solving problems, and constantly improving. That's the Simon I admire. I also admire the Simon who takes responsibility and doesn't shy away from adversity. The one who stands up for his moral values has those difficult conversations, and does the right thing, even when it's unpleasant. Not everyone would pick up the phone and apologise to their creditors, but I did it anyway because ultimately, it was the right thing to do.

I've come to appreciate the fact that I'm willing to share my deepest inner vulnerabilities on a public platform. Social media can be a toxic landscape of comparison, envy, and jealousy. It can damage self-esteem when we only see the glamorous side of others' lives. I'm not suggesting that we should air all our dirty laundry online, but by using my platform and my story as a reality check, I feel like I can offer balance and truth to those who might otherwise see me as an award-winning, Dragons' Den TV star entrepreneur, if I chose to portray myself that way. What's the point of being on TV if you don't use it for something greater than an investment pitch? I'm proud of the Simon who takes on this role and shows both sides of the story.

I never want to be content because I always want to be on the hunt for improvement, no matter how successful I become. Perfection is an unattainable goal, and I prefer it that way. I find my calm in various emotions - whether it's happiness, fear, tragedy, or joy. Staying calm isn't easy when the world around you is chaotic, but that's what I'm working on the most. When I feel angry, upset, excited, euphoric, or frustrated, I ask myself one question. *Can you stay calm?*

Can you enjoy it without getting carried away, Simon? Can you deal with this stress without getting too down, Simon?

Stay calm. Recognise and love yourself. Don't be too hard on yourself.

I've learned that large parts of this feeling, this calmness and clarity is most likely because of the medication I take. As someone who has never really believed much in medication, it's been awakening for me. I can't tell you how many times I told people that I wouldn't be able to feel better until the circumstances changed. It's the circumstances that are causing my mind to crumble, so unless the circumstances change, what can a tablet do about that? A tablet can't put money in my bank, can it? A tablet can't find me sales. That's what I thought. But I was wrong. It can. Because taking that pill has given me the calmness to be able to accept a job driving a taxi for what it is. That puts money in my bank. Without that clear space in my mind and the ability to look at things from a calmer, less chaotic space, I believe I would still be sitting here now in a state of panic about our finances. I don't want to be medicated forever and I hope at some point, my growth will reach a point where I feel able to step away from it, but if I can't, that's okay. A medicated, calm life is a safer and more loving place for myself, my wife and my children.

As I write this closing chapter, there's no Porsche parked

in my driveway. I apologise to any readers who were hoping for that kind of ending. But that's perfectly fine. I'm 38 years old, and I believe I have a long life ahead of me. I intend to live it to the fullest. I've learned to welcome and acknowledge the moments of despair that sometimes sweep through my life, like suicidal sorrows clearing a room of its furniture. I'll acknowledge them and then let them pass, like clouds in the sky.

I may not have a Porsche, but I have something even more valuable. I have my brand, and it's in my hands. I have a job, which may be temporary or could turn into something more permanent. I don't know. I'm just grateful I have it right now. I have a fulfilling hobby in gardening. I play football and was recently appointed the new captain of my Monday night 7-a-side team. I've become someone who has helped hundreds of people, complete strangers, going through debt problems, marriage difficulties, and addiction recoveries. Most importantly, I have this book, which is my greatest achievement. I wrote a book! I accomplished a life-long ambition as a result of one of the darkest moments in my life. If that's not a lesson, I don't know what is.

My daughters, my friends, my family, and my peers will all have this story long after I'm gone. I hope that people can recognise parts of themselves in my story and find inspiration in it. We, as creatives, are often obscure, different, and insecure. We don't fit neatly into society's boxes, and we can be incredibly hard on ourselves. But you know what we are? We're fighters. We're winners. We're dreamers. We're stubborn. We may not be straightforward, but why would we want to be?

Lauren recently asked me if I ever truly believed the business would fail. I told her, 'No.' Deep down, I never did. I may have said it had failed, but I didn't truly mean it. I wanted it to fail at times so I could run away from it, but I couldn't. I couldn't let it fail. That story will only end, if it ever does, on my terms. There was always a small part of me that knew that tomorrow was a new day. Maybe it was that small part of me that prompted me to send that text to Lauren, telling her I was beaten. I needed her to rescue me, for tomorrow.

Hand Dyed Shoe Co. is not just a business; it's a part of me. It's in my very essence. I hope it achieves the greatness I always envisioned for it, and I can repay Dan and Bill for their kindness along the way. I hope it grows into a cultural hallmark representing creative expression and individualism, two things I'm genuinely passionate about. But, in my calm state of mind, I've come to accept that even if it can't grow beyond making just 10 pairs of shoes a month, that's okay. It might be enough to pay the studio rent and keep the dream alive for another month. That, in itself, is still a success. In the meantime, I'll find other ways to earn a living, and that's okay too. I will take it in my stride.

I will always be ambitious and want to do things that are beyond the norm. I like to push boundaries and force change and growth, both economically and personally. I want to do things that scare me and live large parts of my life outside of my comfort zone. It's exciting. There's a thrill in living life like this. I want to jump out of planes and scuba dive. I want to visit countries that aren't your everyday holiday spots. I want to meet people who are unique and have stories to tell. I want to drive a car that is weird and different from the cars my friends drive. I want to show my girls that your upbringing doesn't define your future. You can do whatever you want in life - there are no such things as working-class or upper-class today. You make your own class. Go get it! The only thing that gets in your way is yourself.

I'll never regret opening up about bankruptcy. How can I? Doing that secured our home and brought me an incredible investor into the business. I turned up to football the following Monday and was greeted by one of the lads at the door. He shook my hand. I didn't know what for at first. He congratulated me on my post, which felt weird, but rewarding. He went on to tell me how he was declared bankrupt a while ago and was currently going through the same shit. He took solace from my openness and felt safe enough to be able to share his story with me. Can you imagine how he felt? He had probably never told anybody outside of his immediate family up until that moment. Another lad stopped me a month or two later and told me in the middle of a football match that it was a privilege to play football with me and that the things I post about on social media have helped him massively. I had no idea. He later told me he had been a huge cocaine addict and had overdosed not long before he joined the football group. He said his ego would never allow him to talk about it, let alone post about it. I stopped him in his tracks and asked him what he had just done - he'd talked about it, to me. So, he could do it, if the setting was right for him, ego or no ego. I met a friend of a friend at a funeral of all places who I'd not seen for a long time but we were connected on Facebook. She told me that her business was in trouble and that she didn't know what she was going to do. We exchanged numbers and I told her to call me whenever she wanted to chat and if or when it felt too much. She did, and we chatted for nearly 90 minutes. I guided her through my story and introduced her to Peter. She's on her own journey to recovery now and I know she's going to be absolutely fine. There are so many stories I could tell, which for me makes opening up about my fragility worth it. I'm not proud of what happened, but I'm proud of how I've handled it and how I've used the story for greatness, rather than allowing it to pass me by pretending it never happened. That's why this book is, and will always be my greatest achievement.

As I was writing the closing chapter of Soled Out!, I was

thinking hard about whether the words I had written were any good or of use to anyone. I questioned whether I'd included enough anecdotal masterpieces or if there were any pearls of wisdom in there. In the end, I concluded that I began writing this book for me first as a form of therapy and it has helped me immensely by documenting this journey. That will always be this story's greatest success. I'd encourage anyone to do the same. Only you can decide if you have found value in my story. All I can say is that I have written it from the heart and I've left very few stones unturned when it comes to opening up about what many may perceive as private and personal matters. My hope with that is that if nothing else, the book is authentic and honest. Soled Out! is an insight into the mind of a normal bloke trying to achieve an ambition within the world of entrepreneurialism. I hope you too feel as 'normal' as I do having drawn similarities from the emotional ride that most of us go on during a lifetime. It really is okay not to be okay all of the time.

You'll be pleased to know that I wrote that paragraph from a place of conclusion, as opposed to insecurity.

What happens from here remains a mystery. If only we had a crystal ball. I hope that my book sells one or two copies and that people enjoy it whilst getting something from it. I hope my grandad is watching down from somewhere and he is pleased with how I've grown and the man that I've become. I hope I am, in some way, a reflection of the man I so dearly loved throughout the time we shared.

I still want a Porsche. But for now, I am content enjoying my morning coffee by the dining room window, watching the songbirds and feeding the jackdaws.

Daisy and Penny

You are the most amazing, loving girls I could have ever hoped for. You and your wonderful mam, you all saved me. Thank you. Your warm hearts and open minds were the single biggest reason that I found the strength and encouragement to get through this story. But, more importantly than that, you are the reason I decided to go public with it and write this book.

I need you to know that life is not laid out for us on the day we are born. You can be knocked sideways in life within the blink of an eye. What was your destiny yesterday becomes nothing more than a memory thanks to a chance meeting, an unexpected draw of imagination, or the simplest of actions such as answering a random phone call. Nothing is guaranteed and life will deliver you great days, and unfortunately, terrible days. I wish I could protect you from the worst of it, but I can't, so you will have to learn as you go, just like I did.

One thing that is guaranteed is that at some point, we will all experience enormous emotional pain. You will have moments in your life where nothing can be any worse. You will have days where all perspective and reality will leave your mind and your thoughts go to unwelcome and unhelpful places. It might not be just a day. It will feel like a thousand volts of electricity are frying your brain, cell by cell. Where you find yourself feeling empty and the clarity of your thoughts feel no more than a tiny puff of smoke amongst a raging wildfire. This is okay. It's all okay. Expect it. Welcome it. It is normal to have those thoughts where you consider death as an option; there's nothing wrong with you for thinking them, you're merely getting closer to your only real option which is to recover, learn and grow. Having a broken mind can be as debilitating as having a broken leg, so don't put yourself under so much pressure to walk on day one. Welcome the pain like you would joy and be excited about how you will come back from this moment. Your future will be far greater once the pain has eased, I promise. Be excited about how you will tell your story, just like I have. The room will be black and you will be scurrying around, trying to find the answers in the dark. You don't have to. All you have to find is the smallest flicker of light and move towards it. Grab it. The only thing you have to do is be honest and share your pain with those close to you. Share it with me for as long as I'm here. Don't sugarcoat it. I will always be here for you and I won't ever judge you.

Once you have opened your heart with honesty, your recovery is already well underway. I have seen many people allow pain to consume them. They live their lives into old age carrying bitterness, anger, frustration, disappointment, or worst of all, regret. Nothing makes me sadder than to see this. Don't let this be you. Don't regret anything. Own it. True happiness starts with true honesty.

My beautiful girls, this book is my gift to you. This is my authentic, honest story of how I hit rock bottom but more importantly, how I survived to write the tale.

I love you, more than the whole wide world, and unconditionally.

Daddy x

Made in the USA
Columbia, SC
10 October 2023

7ff44e33-a062-4f5d-b7f7-f72a5a75833aR01